Educational Linguistics - TESOL
University of Pennsylvania
Graduate School of Education
3700 Walnut Street/C1
Philadelphia, PA 19104

Questions of Intonation

**Gillian Brown, Karen L. Currie
and Joanne Kenworthy**

UNIVERSITY PARK PRESS BALTIMORE

©1980 Gillian Brown, Karen L. Currie and Joanne Kenworthy
Published in North America by
UNIVERSITY PARK PRESS
233 East Redwood Street
Baltimore, Maryland

Library of Congress Cataloging in Publication Data

Brown, Gillian.
    Questions of intonation.

    Bibliography: p. 198
    1. Intonation (Phonetics)   I. Currie, Karen L.,
joint author.   II. Kenworthy, Joanne, joint author.
III.   Title.
P222.B76   414   79-2560
ISBN 0-8391-1467-2

Printed and bound in Great Britain

CONTENTS

PREFACE

The work on which this study is based was supported by SSRC grant HR3601 for four years, 1975 to 1979.

We are grateful to the Scottish Education Department for allowing us access to schools, and to the head teachers of Gillespie's High School and Boroughmuir School for allowing us to work with their sixth-year students.

We have been helped most generously by many members of staff as well as by laboratory staff and postgraduate students of the Department of Linguistics, University of Edinburgh. Particularly helpful contributions have been made by John Anthony, Keith Brown, Laurie Iles, Roger Lass and John Laver. Others, from outside Edinburgh, who have offered constructive criticism are David Brazil, Alan Cruttenden, Robin Fawcett, Tony Fox and Stephen Isard. Roger Brown, who worked on the intonation project for six months, contributed particularly to the study of 'paratones'. George Yule, who joined the project in its last year, has worked critically through the text of this work and considerably improved it. Mrs Isobel Atkinson, the secretary to the project, has dealt efficiently with a most difficult manuscript. It is a pleasure to record our thanks to all of them, and also to all the people who acted as our subjects and actually produced the data.

We owe an intellectual debt to many scholars who have ploughed the intonation field before us, particularly to Dwight Bolinger, Wallace Chafe, David Crystal, Michael Halliday and Kenneth Pike.

Division of labour: Karen Currie is responsible for the development of the pause-defined unit and contour analysis described in Chapter 3, and for the experimental work on tonics described in Chapter 5.

Joanne Kenworthy is responsible for the analysis of interaction in Chapter 4, and for the investigation and experimental work on questions in Chapter 6.

Gillian Brown is responsible for trying to fit the pieces together into a coherent framework and for writing up this study. In some cases the results of work done by Currie and Kenworthy have been re-interpreted and added to in the process of writing up. Rather than detail the divergences of interpretation, which in some cases are considerable, the

reader is recommended to consult Currie, 1977, 1978, 1979 and
forthcoming, and Kenworthy, 1977 and 1978.

Transcriptional Conventions

Impressionistic intonational transcription is represented
on a stave. Pauses are represented by + or, if the pause is long,
by ++ in the orthographic transcription. Each extract is
followed by a cypher identifying the subject who spoke the
cited text.

1.0. Introduction

This is a report of ongoing research which is examining the forms and functions of intonation in Scottish English. A number of different accents of Scottish English have been studied in the course of this research. The one which we describe here is that which we have examined in greatest detail — the English spoken by natives of Edinburgh (ESE — Edinburgh Scottish English). We make occasional comparisons with RP (the form of speech which has been most extensively described by British scholars) and with other Scottish English accents but, except when otherwise stated, we shall be concerned to describe ESE.

There are, we believe, advantages in studying the intonation of an accent which has not already accumulated a heavy load of description, as RP has. We began our investigations with few preconceptions other than an expectation that the intonation of ESE must be, in most particulars, similar to that of other English accents since, in general, speakers from different accent areas manage to communicate with each other fairly comfortably. Certainly we expected that the phonetic forms of intonation would vary considerably from one accent to another, and so they do. We find some phonetic variation even within Edinburgh, and startling differences in the typical intonation of Edinburgh and Glasgow (characterised in 1.4.). Our expectation was, and remains, that whereas the phonetic form may vary, the functions that intonation performs will be very similar from one accent of English to the next.

1.1. The Aims of the Study

One of our aims was to characterise the shape of a 'typical' Edinburgh intonation pattern — the sort of intonation pattern that a mimic assumes in 'putting on' an Edinburgh accent. We describe this characteristic pattern in 1.4.

A much more far-reaching aim was to characterise the contrastive intonation patterns of ESE. This apparently simple aim in fact contains hidden assumptions. It assumes that there is a known domain of contrast and it assumes that it is also known what it is that a given contrast 'means'. We established contrasts in three domains: (i) contours whose domain is the pause-defined unit (see Chapter 3), (ii) relative pitch height whose domain is a stressed word and (iii) terminal tones whose domain is the last stressed syllable in a pause-defined unit, together with any following unstressed syllables. You will observe that we do not identify a system of contrasts in a domain that is directly relatable to the notion of 'nucleus' or 'tonic', a very well-established notion in British descriptions of intonation. This is because we found it impossible to identify tonics in our data in a consistent and principled way. We explore the reasons for this at length in Chapter 5.

The second hidden assumption, that of knowing what a given contrast means, has to be expounded in terms of the systems that intonation is realising. Most discussion of intonation function in English has assumed that intonation realises one particular expressive system in language. Thus Jones (1962) is particularly interested in how intonation distinguishes statements from different question-types. O'Connor and Arnold (1959) and Uldall (1964) are particularly interested in the use of intonation to express affective or attitudinal meaning. Halliday (1967) is particularly interested in the way in which intonation reveals information structure. Brazil (1978) is particularly interested in the way participants in a conversation use intonation to control interactive structure. We believe that all these approaches are justified and that intonation participates in the expression of all of these systems. Indeed, we wish to add yet another system to these, that which uses intonation to mark whether a speaker is continuing with an already established topic and that which marks that he is instituting a new topic. Intonation is multi-functional, in the sense that the really very limited resources of pitch patterning are exploited by all these different systems simultaneously. In Chapter 2 we try to disentangle the strands and to distinguish the effects which these systems have on intonation configurations. In Chapter 3 (3.6.ii) we examine in detail the intonation of an extract from a conversation, and attempt to demonstrate there how the variation of intonation can be attributed to the operation of these systems. In Chapter 4 we explore some aspects of interactive marking in intonation and in Chapter 6 we try to tease apart the agglomeration of ideas which results in the notion of 'question intonation'.

One of the main problems which confronts students of intonation is finding external evidence to bring to bear to justify one analysis rather than another. Obviously this problem is particularly acute when one tries, as we have tried, to describe the effect of the interaction of several different systems in spontaneous speech. Since we are interested in spontaneous natural speech we cannot hold several parameters constant and investigate the effect of varying one at a time. Necessarily, then, much of our argument is tentative since it is by no means always possible to bring external evidence that is clearly relevant to bear on the point that is being argued. Naturally we have tried to externalise the argument as much as possible. A good deal of our discussion is supported by instrumental measurements. We point out, even as we use them in presentation, the dangers of relying too heavily on instruments which, whatever their value in terms of reliability, do not listen to speech in the way that naive speakers do. In all cases all material presented here, whether instrumentally analysed or not, is auditorily analysed by two analysts working independently. When we have encountered particular difficulties in interpreting our data confidently, we have appealed to other judges, not only to phonetician colleagues but also to native speakers. We have detailed in the text where external appeals of this sort were made. None the less, in spite of these limited attempts to provide external bolstering evidence, much of the argument is, at the time of writing, unsupported. Our aim, in this period of research, has to be to look for external support. We are nowhere near the state of being able to formulate refutable hypotheses. It is because we are aware that we ask more questions than we are able to answer that we have called this study *Questions of Intonation.*

1.2. The Data

The data on which this study is based is drawn from a series of over one hundred interviews with speakers of ESE, speakers who were born in Edinburgh and had lived throughout their lives in Edinburgh. The subjects include members of a working men's club, a ladies' bowling club, students in their last year at school and at university, professional people in Edinburgh, and people working at the University of Edinburgh (but not members of the academic staff or postgraduate students*).

*The reason for this exclusion is that it seems possible that the speech of those who spend a large proportion of their time immersed in written language may be quite untypical of the speech community as a whole.

The interview was divided into different sections. In the first section subjects were asked to answer a short questionnaire. The first questions needed short answers (name, address, etc.) and later questions required longer answers including lists (names of siblings/children, schools attended, route to work or school). In the second section subjects were asked to read a short text aloud (the text discussed in Chapter 3). In later interviews subjects were then asked to read a list of isolated sentences aloud. The last formal section of the interview consisted of showing the subject a photograph taken in 1855 of part of Edinburgh and asking the subject if he could work out where the photograph was taken from. Many subjects took quite a long time to do this, commenting on their thought processes as they did so, and beginning to ask Karen Currie (the interviewer in all cases) questions about the photograph. Most subjects assumed, when they had finished talking about the photograph, that the interview was completed, and began talking to Karen on other topics — in many cases, especially with older people, about the changes in Edinburgh over the years. These post-interview conversations often lasted for ten or fifteen minutes.

Besides these conversations which took place in the context of an interview, we have recordings of conversations between groups of students in their own homes and between a group of men in a club. We also have recordings of a series of 'games' played by two players where one player was given the text of a short story and the second was given a list of characters and a list of events and asked to reconstruct the story asking his interlocutor only questions which could be answered by 'yes' or 'no'.

The data ranges from the formal readings of texts and sentences in isolation, which produce chunks of speech which can readily be compared, to answers to the questionnaire which, in many cases, produce sequences which are directly comparable. It includes conversation directed by the interviewer, spontaneously produced conversation, and the question-answer sentences produced in playing games.

It may seem that this is quite a wide range of data and that this, combined with the wide range of age, social standing and educational attainment of our subjects, should give us a fairly adequate indication of the possibilities of exploitation of intonation in Edinburgh speech. It is important to realise that this is not the case. There are at least two major objections to this view. The first is that all our data is derived from co-operative adult speech. We have no examples of people being rude to each other, trying to score points off their interlocutors, having violent quarrels or disagreements or protesting undying devotion. Our speakers are not sarcastic or sad or frightened or excited. They all behave in a pleasant, cheerful and co-operative manner. Our data in fact seems reasonably representative of the way most people talk in their public lives, away from home and family and close friends, when they are at work, talking to someone in a shop or chatting while waiting for the bus. This characteristic of the data, as being primarily social, interactive talk, constitutes its second obvious limitation; speakers take up a turn in a conversation of this kind without, in most cases, being sure what they are going to say and at what point they want to end. In most cases they are saying things that they have not said before, expressing opinions that they have not expressed before. This style of speech must be contrasted with speech which is at least partly 'pre-rehearsed' in the sense in which a lecture or sermon or public address is. Occasionally we have an example of a speaker launching into a brief narrative, for instance an account of something that happened on holiday, in which the speaker produces a clearly flowing sequence of events leading up to a pre-determined point. In general, though, most of our data is not 'goal-directed' in this way. Non-goal-directed speech is typologically distinct from goal-directed speech in several respects: it tends to paratactic syntax rather than hypotaxis, it tends to pausing and constant restructuring and substitution of lexis, it tends to add a new item to the topic and then comment on its relevance — a reversal of the paradigm 'given/new' information structure. All of this has an effect on the intonation of this style of speech, an effect we shall discuss in this study.

The data we describe is, in fact, very limited in style. It is co-operative adult speech which is, for the most part, non-goal-directed speech.

A certain amount of our discussion is based on texts read aloud (particularly in the early sections of Chapter 3). The value of texts read aloud is quite simply that they yield speech which can be readily compared from one speaker to the next. However, the relationship between the intonation of texts read aloud and spontaneous speech needs to be carefully investigated. In reading texts the speaker is merely articulating structures which have been pre-prepared. His intonation is 'post-syntactic' and does not arise from the sorts of constraints which apply when speech is produced spontaneously. When subjects are asked to read a text aloud, a co-text gradually develops which does impose constraints on interpretation. None the less the task is not comparable to producing speech and it is noticeable that even highly literate adults perform in it with very varying competence. A reader-aloud first has to assign an interpretation to the text and then to utter it in a way consistent with his interpretation. This is a very different task from the normal processes of speech production in non-goal-directed speech where the speaker has to organise what he wants to say as he is speaking. It must be clear that claims made about intonation on the basis of the study of texts read aloud, should be subject to the most careful scrutiny if there is any suggestion that these will correctly characterise the intonation of spontaneous speech.

1.3. 'Core' Intonation

One of the features which is striking as one listens to our data is the narrow range of variation in intonation. In the type of speech we have recorded, speakers do not produce very varied intonation patterns. Is this to be considered a feature of the accent, or a feature of the group of individuals who are our subjects, or a feature of the style of speech we have recorded?

As far as we can tell, in speech situations similar to those we have recorded for ESE, speakers of other accents do not produce much variation in their intonation. Our recordings of Glasgow, Thurso and RP speakers show no wider variation in this style of speech than ESE.

It seems reasonable to suppose that some individuals are more sensitive to the manipulation of intonation than others. Just as we find considerable variation between individuals in their sensitivity to other aspects of language and their ability to manipulate it effectively (in telling jokes, making puns, seeing ambiguities, writing poetry) so, we surmise, there will exist a similar variation between speakers in their ability to use intonation elaborately. It does not, however, seem reasonable to suppose that all the speakers in our sample are insensitive to the stylistic exploitation of intonation.

Our conclusion must be that speakers do not attempt to extend their use of intonation resources in the style of speech that we have studied. Our expectation is that in a different social setting a wider range of intonation may be encountered. There are social occasions when speakers can 'play' with intonation, just as they can play with other aspects of language, syntax or lexis. Conversations between people who know each other well and enjoy the ritual of 'witty badinage' are obvious examples of such occasions.

We regard the intonation we describe here as 'core intonation', 'core' in that it seems to be the base requirement for an individual to function as a normal member of the speech community. This core intonation can be described in terms of a relatively simple framework, as we hope to show. We assume that any variation we encounter in other social situations can be regarded as elaboration on this core.

1.4. A Taxonomy of Intonation Types

Our intention in this section is to characterise the main differences between a typical neutral intonation pattern of ESE and a typical neutral intonation pattern of RP, an accent which has been so well described by so many scholars. The notion of 'typical' neutral intonation pattern' is difficult to justify though it has clearly been assumed in most descriptions of intonation (see Pike's notion of 'intonation minimum', 1945).* It is a very abstract concept. Obviously such a pattern would not arise in normal speech where it must necessarily be subject to the effect of turn-taking, topic structure and information structure. It is an abstract concept in just the same way that the 'characteristic' articulation of a segment in English, say of /b/, is an abstract concept.

It seems possible to characterise the typical intonation pattern of the accents of English which we have studied in terms of the following variables:

1. The relationship of a base-line of unstressed syllables to stressed syllables.
2. The inclination of the base-line.
3. The type of excursion for stressed syllables (stepped or contoured).

In ESE and RP the base-line regularly occurs lower in pitch than the stressed syllables, which are perceived as higher in pitch. In Glasgow Scottish English, on the other hand, the base-line is raised above the stressed syllables which occur as scoops down in pitch from this raised base-line, yielding the characteristic rising-contour pattern of Glasgow (and Belfast) intonation. In ESE the base-line remains quite flat throughout the intonation pattern, whereas in RP the base-line is inclined so that unstressed syllables earlier in an intonation unit are

*The notion of 'characteristic' contour is well established in the literature, in the 'funnel' and 'tube' shapes proposed for West African tone languages (Welmers, 1959) and the 'hat' contour proposed for Dutch by t'Hart and Cohen (1973).

perceived as being uttered on a higher pitch than unstressed syllables later in the unit (see Figure 1.1 below). In ESE the excursions from the base-line on stressed syllables involve relatively little pitch movement ('steps') compared with the amount of pitch movement on RP stressed syllables ('contours'). (See Figure 1.1.)

In Figure 1.1 we represent a generalised contour where ABCD are stressed syllables and EFG are unstressed syllables, (a) for ESE and (b) for RP:

Figure 1.1

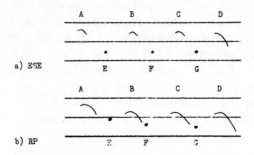

Note that, in ESE, each stressed syllable except the last produces about the same degree of pitch excursion — this means that no single stressed syllable emerges as being perceptually more prominent than the others. In RP, the initial excursion on A and the extended excursion on D contribute to the relative prominence of these items. Note also that the ESE pattern finishes on a slightly extended fall to just below the middle of the pitch range whereas the RP pattern finishes with a fall to low.

2.0. Systems Which Exploit Intonation

One of the major problems in the analysis of intonation is that the speaker exploits the resources of intonation in realising several different systems, all of which may be realised within the same tone unit. For instance a speaker may simultaneously wish to express deference, respond to a question initiating a new topic, and introduce new lexical material into his reply. Each of these very different systems will influence the intonation of the utterance.

In the first sections of this chapter we enumerate those systems which obviously exploit intonation. We cannot possibly deal with each of these exhaustively. In most cases we select only one or two instances to represent the entire system — in the cases of affective meaning we only discuss the speaker's increased involvement with what he is saying. Each of these systems opens up extensive areas of discussion and our procedure has simply been to select for attention that part of the system which we have constantly to take account of in the analysis of our data.

After a rapid overview of the relationship holding between intonation and stress in 2.6., we proceed to 2.7. to demonstrate in an informal way how the different systems interact on the very limited resources of intonation to produce remarkably varied intonational configurations.

2.1. Affective Meaning or Attitude

Intonation has often been held to express affective meaning. It is important, in considering this difficult area, to distinguish between the affective meaning that may be said to derive from a particular intonation pattern and the meaning of the lexical items chosen to illustrate the effect of different intonation patterns. Halliday (1963) exemplifies the different attitudinal effects of two intonation contours thus:

Tone 3: non-commital   – //3<u>six</u>/foot// 3 <u>I</u> don't know//
Tone 5: committed   – //I <u>cer</u>tainly/do//

It is impossible to evaluate the claims made for intonation if the lexis alone implies the distinction being drawn.

A further complication arises with the interplay of features which are centrally held to be intonational features (variation in the pitch of the voice, amplitude, duration) and the set of features which may be subsumed for our immediate purposes under the general heading of 'voice quality'.* Pike (1945) suggests that the sentence <u>You really are</u> <u>a bully aren't you</u> can be identified either as a friendly tease or as an insult, on the basis of the intonation pattern. There are always problems associated with assigning affective meanings to constructed sentences cited out of context but, this aside, it is difficult to create the distinction Pike suggests if the intonation alone is manipulated, and the voice quality is held constant. On the other hand, it is possible to make a very clear distinction between an insult and a friendly tease by holding the intonation constant and manipulating the voice quality. Then the insult is spoken with tense pharynx, raised larynx and no smile on the speaker's face (the lip-spreading will of course have an acoustic effect, particularly on vowel quality) whereas the friendly tease is uttered with breathy voice and a smile. The manipulation of voice quality seems to be a much better indicator of attitude than intonation alone. As Lyons (1977) remarks: 'what is commonly referred to as tone of voice summarises the most important of vocal features with a modulating function; and the frequency with which one hears the remark "It's not what he said but the way he said it" testifies to the recognition by listeners of their importance'.

There seems to be a small number of intonation patterns which are conventionally related to a set of attitudes. Thus a speaker who wishes to be kindly and encouraging to his interlocutor will tend to use frequent intonation patterns with final rises, associated with a 'kindly' voice quality. This type of pattern occurs mainly, in our data, on the <u>mhms</u> which one speaker utters while another is talking. Similarly other quite different attitudes like 'politeness' and 'hectoring' are often associated with rising intonation patterns when accompanied by the appropriate modulations of voice quality and situated in appropriate contexts.

There are also intonational effects arising from more obvious

*For detailed discussion of the interaction of intonational features and other 'paralinguistic vocal features' see Crystal, 1969; Laver, 1968; Brown, 1977.

physiological changes in the speaker. Thus any speaker who is moved by strong emotion, surprise or anger, will, if he does not control it, find his pitch span extended upwards in his voice range. There are rather few examples of this in our data, since relaxed co-operative conversation is not conducive to drama. However some examples clearly demonstrate surprise, which is marked by a shift into the speaker's high pitch range:

Figure 2.1

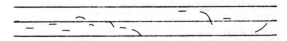

A. I   had a Harvey Wallbanger   B. did you what's that (23 CM)

The attitudinal effect which we will treat as representative of this system is that which arises when a speaker suddenly becomes much more involved with what he is saying and speaks more animatedly. This is regularly marked by a raising of the speaker's pitch range which lasts throughout a complete utterance (pause-defined unit; see discussion in 3.6.). There is a problem in determining the domain of what we describe as being influenced in such a way. It may be the case that a particular speaker is nervous throughout the interview, with consequent raising of pitch range and reduction of pitch span. Our procedure is to establish a normal range for a speaker throughout the interview and establish a normal base-line of unstressed syllables (see 3.3.i and 3.6.iv) and then note deviations from this norm. Where a speaker raises one or two words high in his pitch range within an utterance but returns to within his normal base-line range, we treat this as emphasis and discuss it within the information system (see 2.4.). Where a speaker raises the whole of an utterance, including the unstressed syllables, we may attribute this to the realisation of affective meaning or attitude (see discussion in 2.7.v).

There are expressions of other attitudes in our data — uncertainty, and amusement, for instance, occur on several occasions. However, for the purpose of this study the only consistent reference to this system of attitudinal expression will be in terms of the increased involvement of the speaker in what he is saying.

2.2. Interactional Structure

Intonation is used to mark co-operation between speakers in structuring a discourse. Thus, in 4.1., we show that a speaker who embarks on a new topic by asking a question about it, begins his utterance high in his pitch range. This is accounted for in our discussion of topic-structure (2.3.). However, the second speaker, answering the question, also begins his utterance high in his pitch range, whereas, when a speaker asks a question on an already established topic low in his pitch range, the second speaker will reply to it low in his pitch range. This echoing by the second speaker of the first speaker's placing in the pitch range and, hence, assessment of the topic structure of the discourse they are jointly embarked on, has to be explained in terms of co-operation by the second speaker with the first.

Intonation is also used as one of the cues which shows that a speaker is anxious to continue his turn in the conversation or is willing to give up his turn. It is often the case that a speaker who utters a complete syntactic structure and so might be deemed to have finished his turn, none the less produces the last stressed item in his structure with a not-low terminal (see 6.4.) as a marker that he wishes to continue.

There appear to be two main strategies available to speakers for giving away turns. When the speaker seems to have exhausted all he has to say on a topic he may tail away syntactically, intonationally and in volume, producing constant pauses and repetition:

Figure 2.2

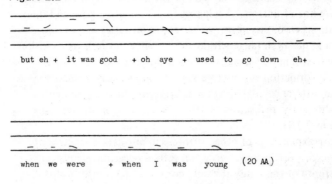

but eh + it was good + oh aye + used to go down eh+

when we were + when I was young (20 AA)

A quite different strategy of giving-away a turn arises when a speaker wishes the next speaker to continue speaking on the same topic that he himself is speaking on. In many cases he will produce a question, which clearly has the function of determining the topic of the next speaker's utterance. In the sequence below we illustrate two speakers co-operatively finishing off one topic and then initiating another (related) topic:

Figure 2.3

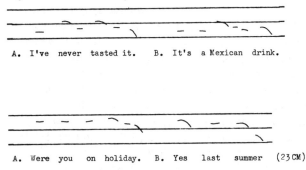

A. I've never tasted it.   B. It's a Mexican drink.

A. Were you on holiday.   B. Yes last summer   (23 CM)

Where one speaker shows that he is tired of a topic, by depressing his pitch span and sinking lower in his pitch range, the second speaker may co-operate in finishing off the topic. If the interaction is not then to finish, the speakers have to co-operate in establishing a new topic. Note that what is at issue here is the co-operation between the speakers. It is clear that this sort of co-operation has an effect on the intonation of utterances which occur in real contexts of discourse.

2.3. Topic Structure

The effect of topic structure on the realisation of intonation is easiest to discern in conversations where individuals have extended turns. In a sequence of very short adjacency pairs it is much less clearly marked. In extended conversation, however, when the participants stop 'feeding' more matter into the topic of a conversation, the end of the topic is typically marked by the repetition of lexical items already introduced (unusual − yes, I think that's true) or by a lexical tail-away on prefabricated phrases: and so on, and things like that, that's how I see it, etc. This fading-away at a lexical level is reflected phonetically by speakers dropping low in their pitch ranges, fading away in amplitude, and leaving a long pause at the end of the turn. If the conversation is to continue, speakers then make an effort to start a new topic. The new beginning usually relates in some way to the here and now, either to the speaker: I've often thought, I suppose, Jim was telling me the other day . . . , When I was . . . , or to the hearer Have you ever wondered why . . . , <u>Was it you who was telling me</u> . . . . The new start is again marked phonetically, this time by the speaker speaking high in his pitch range and speaking loudly (see discussion in 3.6.).

The beginnings and endings of large areas of discussion are often identifiable by the sorts of markers just mentioned and by a clear shift from lexis relating to one topic, to lexis relating to another. However, within these large areas it is possible to discern smaller movements of what is under discussion, where newly introduced items flow on in a manner clearly related to items introduced earlier within the same large structure. There is, at the moment, no available model for discussing these shifts within a topic. In spite of much recent discussion in this area (see for example Grimes, 1975; Li, 1976; Van Dijk, 1977), there remains a problem with the formal identification of topics. It is attractive to suppose that the organisation which we perceive might be able to be expressed in terms of presupposition shifts (see Jackendoff, 1972), where a set of utterances within a 'sub-topic' area shares the same presupposition structure, whereas a shift to a new sub-topic involves some new set (or sub-set) of presuppositions.

This is an area of crucial interest to intonation analysis and is undoubtedly the area of research which needs most urgent attention before an understanding of intonation function can make much headway. In this study we make frequent appeal to the notion of 'sub-topic' change in order to account for pause-length and high initial peaks in intonation contours (see 3.3. and 3.6.). Naturally we attempt to reduce the circularity of the argument at these points by remarking on the introduction of new lexis into the discussion, the reintroduction of a speaker-related filler, <u>I reckon</u>, etc. None the less the strongest indicator that the speaker is changing direction within the overall topic area is generally intonation. The speaker typically organises his speech into 'paratones' — a short sequence of units beginning with a stressed peak high in the speaker's voice range (see 3.6.). These paratones are very much shorter than written paragraphs and, in the style of conversation discussed here, often much shorter than those which occur in formal speech (especially speech that has been to some extent pre-rehearsed).* In general, they are only three or four units long. It seems to us clear that these do reflect the speaker's organisation of the discourse into sub-topics related to the main ongoing topic (see 3.6.).

---

*In the sense that a lecturer may write a lecture before delivering it without referring to his notes. Although he is not reading his text, he has already mentally ordered the arguments and developed the overall structure of what he wishes to say before he begins to speak.

We are uncomfortably aware that, until an independent theory of topic-structure is formulated, much of our argument in this area is in danger of circularity.

We draw an artificial distinction by separating off discussion of topic structure in this section from discussion of information structure in the next section. Everything considered in these two sections is relevant to the speaker's organisation of what he wants to talk about. We make the distinction partly for convenience, and partly in order to focus attention in this section on an area of discourse structure which appears, in general, to have been ignored.

2.4. Information Structure

One of the currently most discussed functions of intonation is the part that it plays in marking the information structure of discourse (see for example Halliday, 1967; Chafe, 1972, 1974, 1976)). A brief account will be given here in terms of the model proposed by Halliday which is followed by a summary of our departure from this model. (A more extended account follows in Chapters 3 and 5.)

Halliday suggests that the speaker organises his speech into units of information which are realised phonetically as *tone groups*. A tone group has a phonetically specifiable contour which is organised around the syllable containing the greatest pitch movement within the tone group, the *tonic* syllable, which forms (part of) the *focused* word in the information unit. Every tone group contains one tonic which may be preceded by a *pre-tonic*, and followed by further words which will continue the direction of pitch initiated in the tonic. The structure of the tone group may be represented thus:

(pre-tonic)   TONIC   (stressed/unstressed items)

In terms of information structure, the tone group is normally (i.e. when 'unmarked') isomorphic with the clause or simple sentence. Marked information structure will yield either two or more tone groups realising one clause or (less commonly) two or more clauses realised in one tone group. The internal organisation of the tone group reflects the decision of the speaker as to which word (or constituent) is focal, 'new', which is marked by the tonic, and which part is 'given', i.e. that not within the domain of the tonic. In unmarked cases, the last lexical item in the tone group will be marked by the tonic as 'new'. In marked cases the tonic appears on some item other than the last lexical item, and in this case any following lexical items are treated by the speaker as given. In decontextualised sentences, readers will be expected to produce tonics on the last lexical item. So in sentences like:

> John's going to London
> Who's pinched my book?
> Those houses were built by my grandfather

the tonic will be expected to fall on the last lexical item in each case (London, book and grandfather). However it can happen in the structure of discourse that the last lexical item is given in the preceding discourse, in which case the tonic moves on to the next lexical item to the left. So in the following simple constructed paradigm the tonic moves to the left if the right-most lexical item is given in the contextualising question:

1. A.   What's happened today?
   B.   Daddy washed the CAR

2. A.   What's happened to the car?
   B.   Daddy WASHED (the car) (it)

3. A.   Who's washed the car?
   B.   DADDY (washed the car), (washed it), (did it), (did)

As the items in parenthesis make clear, the system of tonic placing *(tonicity)* interacts with systems of anaphora. Halliday treats the system of tonicity as one of the formal systems of anaphora.

   Given status may be derived either from having already been mentioned in the preceding discourse or from being physically present in the context of situation. New status may be derived from being introduced into the discourse for the first time, or by being treated differently when introduced a second time (for instance, by being contrasted or questioned). Halliday treats contrastiveness as a kind of 'newness' and points out that an utterance like:

> JOHN painted the shed yesterday

can both be an answer to the question Who painted the shed yesterday? where JOHN is not contrastive, and to the question Did MARY paint the shed yesterday? where JOHN is contrastive. Halliday states that there are no reliable phonetic cues which will distinguish between these two functions.

In all our discussion of those areas of intonation which relate to information structure, we began by using Halliday's model and our debt to him cannot be overemphasised. However, we have been obliged to deviate from his model in several respects. Here follows a brief outline of the particular ways in which our model deviates from Halliday's. In each case a reference is given to the section in this study where we discuss the reasons for our departure:

1. *Tone group.* We cannot consistently identify tone groups by intonational criteria (Chapter 3). We recognise *pause-defined units*, defining *contour units*.

2. *Tonic.* We cannot consistently identify tonics (Chapters 3 and 5). We believe that Halliday's system of tonicity conflates two separate systems: (i) a delimitative system of terminal markers (see 6.4.) and (ii) the information-structure marking system (see 5.4.). We recognise pitch height markers of contrastive/new and given information value and two terminal tones.

3. *Given/new structure.* Much of the spontaneous speech arising in conversations in our data does not display a 'given/new' sequencing, even within units which can confidently be related to Hallidaian tone groups. In many cases the speaker adds a new item to the topic area and then comments on how it relates to the topic (see 3.6.). We do not recognise an unmarked information structure within pause-defined units.

4. *Contrast/Emphasis.* Like Halliday we recognise 'contrast' as being part of the system by which the speaker shows the hearer the relative importance of an item. In our data, speakers appear to distinguish not only between given and new, but also between new and contrast, in that what is contrasted regularly appears on a higher pitch than what is introduced as new which, in turn, appears on a higher pitch than what is introduced as given. However, among the items which are introduced as formal contrasts (i.e. where one item is formally in contrast with a previously mentioned member of the same class) there also appear items raised high in the speaker's pitch range which can be interpreted either as in non-specific contrast or, more straightforwardly, as being *emphasised* by the speaker (see 3.6.).

2.5. Speech Function or Illocutionary Force

It has often been claimed that there is a close relationship between the form of an intonation pattern, in particular whether its end-point rises or falls, and the illocutionary force of an utterance, whether it functions as a statement, question or command. It is generally assumed that statements and commands will be uttered on falling tones and questions, at least polar questions, on rising tones. This view is discussed in Chapter 6 and its relevance to ESE is explored. There we identify two types of terminals in ESE – *low* and *not-low*. Low terminals are regularly associated with the end of topics, with the end of a turn when a speaker has no more to say on a topic, and with conducive questions where the speaker has a high expectation of the correctness of the assumptions that lie behind his question. Low terminals are also frequently associated with non-finality in topic or turn when a speaker indicates that there is more to come on the same topic by some other means, for instance, incomplete syntax (see the extract discussed in 3.6.). Not-low terminals are associated with more to come on the same topic, in the same turn, and with non-conducive questions. Not-low is also associated with a range of affective meanings including deference, politeness, vulnerability (see further discussion in 6.3.).

It is clear that there is no one-to-one relationship between intonation patterns and speech functions. There does, however, seem to be a tendency for conduciveness in questions to be marked by a low terminal and for non-conduciveness in questions to be marked by a not-low terminal.

The figure which summarises the discussion of the tones of ESE in 6.4. is reproduced here to show the variety of realisation of low and not-low terminals. It should be noted that, whereas there are examples of boosted terminals in text-readings, there are no examples of boosted terminals in conversation in our data.

Figure 2.4

	low terminal	not-low terminal
Boost	boost-high-fall-to-low	boost-high-fall-to-mid rise-to-boost-high
Peak	high-fall-to-low	high-fall-to-mid rise-to-high
Depress	mid-fall-to-low low-level	mid-level rise-to-mid

BOOST indicates the pitch at which contrasted/emphasised items are introduced (boost high), PEAK the pitch at which new items are introduced (high) and DEPRESS the pitch at which given items are introduced (mid). 'Low' indicates the base-line. So if the final item in a pause-defined unit is contrasted and topic-final, the contrastiveness will be realised in terms of boosted pitch height and the finality in terms of the low terminal (together with completed syntax, etc.).

2.6. Intonation and Stress

In sections 2.1. to 2.5. we have discussed the systems which exploit the resources of intonation. In this section we pause to examine the relationship between intonation and stress before moving on, in the next section, to look at the effects of these systems of intonation patterns.

The relationship between the terms 'intonation' and 'stress' in the literature is confused and confusing. It is well known that in American work what is called 'primary stress' is what in British studies is called the 'tonic' or 'nuclear' tone in intonation studies. In her extensive study of 'suprasegmentals' in speech, Lehiste (1970) ranges widely across the descriptive, instrumental and experimental literature in order to try to discern a principled means of distinguishing stress from intonation, and encounters the familiar difficulties. The approach we take in this study will be rather high-handed, since we are not primarily concerned with what is usually discussed under 'stress'.

We will assume, following Bolinger (1961) and many others, that words in English have a characteristic stress pattern, and that this characteristic stress pattern forms an intrinsic part of the structure of a word and is essential to its auditory identification. We assume that the stressed syllables of an English word will normally be pronounced with higher pitch than the unstressed syllables.

We will further assume that other terms which include the term 'stress' — like 'primary stress', 'sentence stress' and 'contrastive stress' — all appeal to intonation. That is, we take it that stress is a property of words and that intonation is a property of utterances. Where a single word constitutes a one-word utterance, the word will retain its intrinsic stress pattern, that is its stressed syllable will be uttered with high pitch and its unstressed syllable(s) with lower pitch, but an intonation contour will be superimposed — that is to say, the pitch margins of the word will be affected by the topic- structure and turn-taking structure (at least) of the discourse of which the word forms part. (We shall ignore, for the purposes of this discussion, the complicating factor of those words which are said to have 'secondary stress'.)

Finally, we will assume that, in general, all lexical items (nouns, main verbs, adjectives, adverbs) will have one stressed syllable which is uttered on high pitch when they occur in speech, and that grammatical items (auxiliary verbs, pronouns, etc.) will be unstressed and uttered on low pitch. This is obviously a gross oversimplification. There are some grammatical items, for example deictics like 'that' and 'these' which are frequently stressed. However, for the moment, we make the simplifying assumption that we can distinguish between lexical and grammatical classes and that we will assign one stressed syllable to each lexical item and that everything else will be unstressed (we modify this statement in 3.6.iv). Clearly there are objections to this procedure but it will allow us to make generalisations which will account for a very large number of utterances. In fact, even this simplifying assumption does have to be elaborated in one case only, and then we can handle a lot of discourse in terms of our simple statement. The elaboration is necessary to make it possible to state that polysyllabic grammatical items, which occur in pause-defined units must have a stress structure assigned to them. Thus logical connectors ('however', 'moreover', 'furthermore', etc.) and many 'prefabricated' logically connecting phrases ('not only but also', 'if and only if', etc.) as well as comments by the speaker on his commitment to the truth value of what he is saying ('I think', 'of course', etc.) will frequently appear in pause-defined units by themselves and must be assigned a stress structure.

In the vagaries of performance almost any item can be isolated by itself in a pause-defined unit and bear phonetic cues to stress — be uttered on a high pitch, with extended pitch movement accompanied by considerable duration and amplitude while the speaker 'rests' on this item, holding his turn, as he works out what he wants to say next. We are not attempting to account for this phenomenon.

This brief account of stress in relation to intonation ignores the important contribution of rhythmicality, the patterning of unstressed and stressed syllables within a regular foot-structure, to the structure of utterances in speech. For the most satisfactory account of rhythmic structure in English in relation to RP see Abercrombie, 1964. We do not know of an extended study of the rhythm of Scottish English, which is remarkably different from that of RP. Perhaps the most striking differences arise from the different patterns of cliticisation and the fact that 'long vowels' and diphthongs are realised as phonetically very much longer in RP than they are in ESE.

2.7. A Model for ESE 'Core' Intonation

We have listed a number of systems which exploit intonation in their realisation: (i) affective meaning, (ii) interactional structure, (iii) topic structure, (iv) information structure and (v) speech function. We shall not attempt to discuss here the principles by which a speaker chunks his speech into pause-defined units. We simply assume this chunking. What we are trying to do here is demonstrate the effect of the interaction of these five systems on the intonation of a pause-defined unit.

To begin with, we assign stressed and unstressed values to syllables and then consider the effect of topic structure and information structure.

2.7.i   Stressed and Unstressed Syllables

Stressed syllables are uttered on high pitch and unstressed syllables on low pitch. We recognise two pitch levels:

Figure 2.5

Level 2 _____

Level 1 _____

where level 2 represents the level assigned to stressed syllables and level 1 the level assigned to unstressed syllables, the base-line in ESE. Each level may be raised by a *booster* feature or lowered by a *depress* feature as the five systems each have a simultaneous effect.

A sequence of alternating unstressed and stressed syllables would appear like this:

Figure 2.6

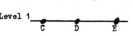

2.7.ii   Information Structure I: Pause-defined Units and Terminals

Pause-defined units are bounded by pauses (see 3.2.). In general, initial unstressed syllables are slightly raised (much less markedly in ESE than in RP. See discussion in 3.6.ii).

The terminals which were discussed in 2.4. have as their domain the last stressed syllable of a pause-defined unit and any following unstressed syllables. The most frequently heard terminal in conversation is not-low, realised as a fall-to-mid. *Mid* will be defined as intermediate between levels 2 and 1.

In some cases two or three complete syntactic structures (clauses or phrases) may occur within a pause-defined unit. On such occasions the speaker sometimes, but by no means always, marks the last lexical item of such a structure with a terminal marker.

If we assign an onset marker and a not-low terminal to the sequence of stressed and unstressed syllables, the effect will be to slightly raise unstressed C, produce a falling contour on stressed B, falling to 2− and to boost unstressed E to 1+. (The effect of depressing 2 and boosting 1 will often, in both cases, produce a pitch at mid.)

Figure 2.7

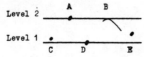

2.7.iii   Information Structure II: Given/New/Contrastive

Contrasted or emphasised items will be boosted to 2+. New lexical items will be introduced at 2. Given lexical items will be depressed to 2−. If the speaker contrasts a grammatical item which would normally occur at level 1, contrastive boost will raise this to 2+, just like a lexical item (see 3.6.).

The effect of information structure on the sequence in Figure 2.7 will depend on how the speaker assigns the statuses contrast/new/given within this structure. If he were to assign contrast to A, this would raise A to 2+. However, let us assume that he assigns new to A and given to B. A then remains at level 2 and B is lowered to 2−. The cumulation of assignment of 2− and not-low terminal realised as fall-to-mid will yield a mid-level tone (which may be very slightly falling):

Figure 2.8

2.7.iv Topic Structure

A new topic or sub-topic introduced into the discourse produces an
initial-peak contour where the first stressed syllable is boosted to 2+
and any preceding unstressed syllables are boosted up to 1+. (There is
a considerable range of perceived pitch variation on unstressed
syllables in topic-initial position. We assume that the range from level
2 to 2– which is significant for stressed syllables is non-significant for
unstressed syllables. Boosting an unstressed syllable to 1+ may imply
that it occurs high in the speaker's voice range.) Note that topic-
structure can boost to 2+ just as contrast can boost to 2+.

In topic-final any unstressed syllable following a final stressed item
with terminal low may be depressed to 1–, below the normal base-line
for the speaker.

If we assign a topic-initial marker to the sequence in Figure 2.8 the
effect will be to boost initial C and to boost A to 2+:

Figure 2.9

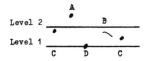

If the speaker intends to speak for some time, continuing on the
same topic, he will often raise the whole of a short unit like this at the
beginning of a topic, yielding a configuration like this:

Figure 2.10

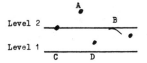

In such a configuration the whole base-line is raised and the stressed peaks are correspondingly boosted. Rather than account individually for the raising of each syllable in such a case, we suggest that when the whole intonational structure of a pause-defined unit is raised in such a way it should be said to be subject to a 'shift-up' in the speaker's pitch range, which preserves the relative pitch distinctions.

We distinguish between shift-up and neutral key, and we take the domain of key to be the pause-defined unit. In 2.7., note that attitudinal involvement may involve a shift-up in key and, in 4.2., that key is a system exploited by speakers in interactive discourse. Once again the limited cues of intonation are exploited by a number of different expressive systems. We can hardly be surprised that, even in context, the 'meaning' of intonation is by no means always clear (see discussion in Yule, forthcoming).

2.7.v   *The Effect of the Other Systems*

The systems we have discussed so far, information structure and topic structure, seem to us fundamental, in that no meaningful utterance can be spoken without reference to these systems. Either what the speaker says relates to an already established topic, or he begins a new topic. Similarly he is obliged to assign contrastive/new/given status to lexical items.

The remaining three systems are essential in describing interactive conversational speech. It is not, however, always necessary to appeal to these systems in describing a monologue. We simply summarise at this point how some fragments of these systems would affect the sequence we have been looking at:

1. *Affective meaning.* The increased involvement of the speaker with what he is saying will be realised by a shift-up in key. This implies a raising in the speaker's pitch range of exactly the sort that we represented in Figure 2.10. (This may or may not be accompanied by paralinguistic vocal features – voice quality adjustments, etc.).
2. *Interactional structure.* (i) If speaker A introduces a topic with a question asked on a shifted-up key, speaker B must also shift-up in key. This, again, will produce a configuration like that in Figure 2.10. (ii) The speaker may choose to indicate 'more to come' and select a not-low terminal, as we have done, or he may select a low terminal to indicate finality.
3. *Speech function.* The speaker may mark a question as conducive by choosing a low terminal or as non-conducive by choosing a not-low

terminal.

It must be clear that the resources of intonation are very limited. These limited resources are exploited by a number of different systems. This necessarily means that the signalling function of intonation is not unambiguous since a single cue, say pitch height at 2+ can be the realisation of an item made prominent by a speaker for any one of several different reasons.

2.7.vi   Tonal Sandhi

So far, our model suggests that we are dealing with sequences of level pitches. As anyone knows, who has listened carefully to intonation (or examined instrumental analyses of it), it is rare to find even short stretches of speech which are heard as being uttered on a series of level pitches (or which yield unchanging instrumental readings). Where then, do the perceived pitch movements arise from? The most obvious source of movements within a pause-defined unit is tonal sandhi, the tendency for the pitch of a syllable at one level to be assimilated to the pitch of a syllable at another level. Thus the margins of each syllable will tend to assimilate towards the margins of adjacent syllables. In the case of an unstressed syllable between two stressed syllables, particularly if the stresses are boosted, the whole unstressed syllable will be raised very considerably in pitch, well above the normal base-line. In the case of a stressed syllable between two unstressed syllables, the stressed syllable will tend to preserve its own height but its margins will be noticeably pulled down towards the flanking lower pitches. This is not, however, a symmetrical effect. That is to say that the pitch of a stressed syllable A, occurring between two unstressed syllables B, yielding a sequence BAB, will not assimilate equally to the pitch of the two unstressed syllables. The level assigned to a syllable appears to be 'placed' earlier rather than later in the syllable (so that, for instance, the highest pitch of a stressed syllable will be perceived as being 'placed' on the initial element of a diphthong). There is, therefore, a greater assimilatory movement of pitch in the final margins of syllables than there is in the initial margins, yielding a characteristic pattern of a short rising onset to the perceived highest pitch and a much longer falling away towards the base-line.* The effect of tonal sandhi on the sequences that we constructed would be to bring them very much

*We are obliged to L.A. Iles for confirming that in speech synthesis a pattern of Fo placement with a short rising onset to a peak and then a longer falling-away yields a perceptually satisfactory stressed syllable.

nearer to the impressionistic transcriptions that we produce throughout this study. Each stressed syllable would be represented as a slight fall preceded by a very small onset-rise, whereas each unstressed syllable would be subject to some phonetic raising in the environment of adjacent high peaks.

There are well-known effects on pitch perception which arise from different segmental environments, so that, for instance, the pitch of a vowel following a voiceless consonant will tend to be perceived as higher than that of a vowel following a voiced consonant (see Ohala, 1978). Similarly nasals, laterals, and formant structure in vowels all affect perceived pitch quality. It is clear that segmental structure contributes importantly to the impression of constant fluctuation of pitch in speech. This degree of variation is simply assumed in the present study.

2.7.vii   The Components of the Model

At a phonological level we recognise the following sets of intonational resources available for the speaker to exploit:

1. *Key*. Shift-up or netural. (The speaker may select shift-up to mark any of the following: the introduction of a new topic, a response to a new topic, animated involvement in what he is saying.)
2. *Contour*. Peak-initial or equal-peak. (The speaker must select peak-initial for topic and sub-topic initial, and equal peak contour for continuation of the same topic.)
3. *Pitch-height*. Boost/peak/depress. (The speaker will mark contrast/ emphasis with boosted height, new with peak height and given with depressed height. Note that boosted height may also arise because of a speaker's shift-up in key.)
4. *Terminal-tone*. Low or not-low. (The speaker may select not-low terminals to mark continuation of his turn or of the topic, kindness, deference etc. Otherwise he will select a low terminal.)

In the rest of this study we shall constantly refer back to these categories as we attempt to justify the model of intonation we have outlined in this chapter. In this discussion we shall, in general, represent examples impressionistically on a three-line stave. The outer lines, A and C, on this stave represent the extremes of the speaker's normal pitch range. The middle line, B, is a convenient reference point. The lines on this stave have no theoretical status. They may be related to levels 1 and 2 (unstressed and stressed levels) in the following way:

Figure 2.11

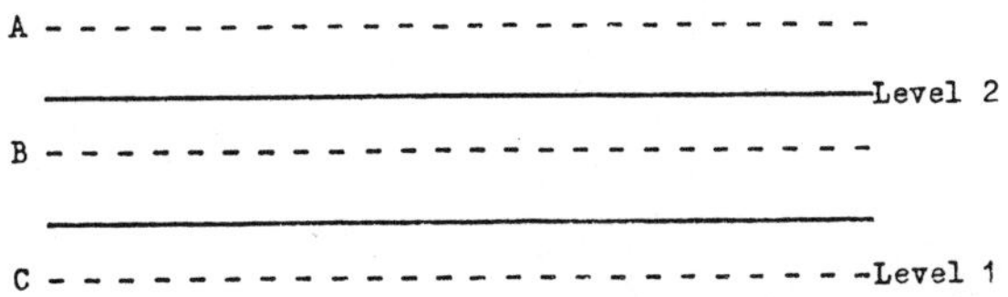

```
A - - - - - - - - - - - - - - - - - - - - - - - -
   ————————————————————————————————————Level 2
B - - - - - - - - - - - - - - - - - - - - - - - -

   ——————————————————————————————————
C - - - - - - - - - - - - - - - - - - - - - -Level 1
```

The convenience of the central line of the three-line stave will be clear. It represents the pitch range where items boosted from level 1 and depressed from level 2 will normally be found. (See further discussion in 3.2.i.)

3.0. Intonation Contours

The units of intonation that we initially attempted to work with are
the *paratone* (discussed in 2.3.), the *tone group* and the *tonic*. Of
these units, those which are generally assumed in discussion of
intonation are the tone group ('tone unit', 'breath group', 'phonemic
clause' — all terms which appear to refer to the same sort of domain)
and the tonic ('nucleus' or 'primary stress'). In listing, as alternatives,
terms from different systems of description, we do not suggest that
the terms are strictly equivalent. What we do assume however is that
the phonetic entity identified by these various terms will be the same
entity. That is we assume that Halliday's 'tone group' will extend over
the same domain as Crystal's 'tone group' and Pike's 'intonation
contour', and that Halliday will identify as the tonic in a tone group
the same item that Kingdon would identify as nucleus and Chomsky as
having primary stress. It should be noted, though, that whereas in
many theories the tonic or primary stress is to be identified in terms of
the phonetic features of a particular syllable or word (pitch height,
pitch movement, duration, intensity, etc.), in Halliday's framework the
configuration of pitch patterns before and after the tonic may
contribute to its identification. A further difference, of course, is that
the functions attributed to units thus identified differ quite widely
from one theory to another and, in this sense, the terms cannot be
regarded as equivalent.

3.1. Tone Groups

We shall, for the moment, adopt Halliday's term 'tone group' for the
unit which is created by the speaker to organise his utterance into units
which have some coherent internal syntactic and semantic structure.
Our problem is to identify these units in the stream of speech. In prose
read aloud most readers will, to a large extent, agree on the tone group
organisation of the text and will produce tone group units which are

comparable to those of other readers, especially where punctuation in the text clearly marks the bounds of such units. In spontaneous speech, however, there are many occasions where no clear indication is given of tone group boundary markers. Halliday is reticent about what would constitute such markers, stating merely that the placing of tone group boundaries is a theoretical decision (Halliday, 1963). It is not clear, from looking at Halliday's own cited examples, how he decides where to place boundaries and to what 'theoretical' aspects he is appealing. Thus he cites an example (Halliday, 1967):

//4   for/<u>some</u>/reason he's//1 gone a/way and he/
hasn't/left an ad/<u>dress</u>//.

If tonality (chunking into tone groups) is held to reflect the speaker's organisation of *information*, it is hard to see why there should be deemed to be a division between 'he's' and 'gone away'. Crystal is more explicit about what constitute tone group boundary markers. He claims (Crystal, 1969) that there are regular definable phonological boundaries for tone groups (units) in speech which is normal, and not too hurried: (i) step-up in pitch (if the nuclear movement is falling), (ii) step-down in pitch (if the nuclear movement is rising) or either a step-up or step-down where the nuclear movement is level. This marking arises, he suggests, because the onset of each tone unit in the speaker's utterance is fairly constant at the same pitch level. Together with 'slight pause', these pitch markers are sufficient to 'indicate unambiguously where a tone-unit boundary should go in connected speech in the vast majority of cases' (1969). He admits that ambiguous cases can be 'thought up' but suggests that in those cases syntactic or semantic criteria will resolve the difficulty and allow a decision to be made.

It is true that in many cases one is able to assign tone group boundaries with some confidence. However, in a very substantial number of cases we encountered problems, not, in general, arising because the speaker was speaking very fast (which Crystal implies is likely to create most difficulties) but because the speaker was trying to work out what he wanted to say as he was saying it, and what he wanted to say was quite difficult for him to express. Thus speakers pause in the middle of noun phrases, extend their pitch span on non-contrastive definite articles, as in <u>the</u> + <u>er</u> + <u>erm</u>+ <u>the</u> + <u>answer</u> <u>might be</u>, meanwhile changing height and pitch direction on 'fillers' which appear to have no other function than to maintain the speaker's

right to speak while he plans his utterance. In many cases we found
that syntactic or semantic criteria would not enable us to make a
principled decision as to where to assign a tone group boundary.
Let us consider some of these cases.

Figure 3.1

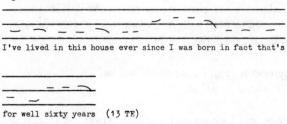

I've lived in this house ever since I was born in fact that's

for well sixty years   (13 TE)

The problem here arises with the phrase in fact. Auditory and
spectrographic analyses show no pauses bounding in fact, and there is
no perceptible pitch change preceding or following it. Pitch movement
on house, born and years suggest that we have at least three tone
groups here. We seem to have three plausible analyses: (i) to suppose
that in fact is included within the second tone group (I've lived here
ever since I was born in fact), (ii) to suppose that it is included within
the third tone group (in fact that's for well sixty years) or (iii) to
decide that in fact constitutes a separate tone group. Appeal to
semantic criteria obviously does not help — indeed, we might have
supposed that the phonetics would have sorted out the semantic
analysis for us here and made it clear what in fact is modifying, but,
as happens frequently in our data, the ambiguity is unresolved.

Figure 3.2

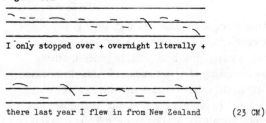

I only stopped over + overnight literally +

there last year I flew in from New Zealand   (23 CM)

The problem here is very similar to the one discussed above. What
does last year modify? Do we analyse it with the first phrase, yielding
I only stopped overnight there last year or with the second, yielding

last year I flew in from New Zealand, or do we suppose that we have a
independent tone group, last year? The problem once again seems to
arise because the speaker is having planning problems. The result is
that it is quite unclear as one listens to the tape of this sequence what
it is that last year is modifying.

This sort of problem arises so frequently in our data that it gives rise
to speculation about the amount of 'work' the speaker is prepared to
do or expects his listener to do in this sort of co-operative talk. It
seems that up to a point the speaker will abide by Grice's (1975)
conversational maxims but, when he is having problems in expressing
himself, he has a fairly high tolerance of, if not ambiguity, at least
unclarity. It seems plausible, too, to suggest that the hearer does not,
in this sort of casual conversation, make an exhaustive analysis of what
the speaker is saying and is not generally consciously aware of this
sort of detail. Certainly we have very few examples of hearers
backtracking over what has just been said to sort out lack of clarity in
cases where *we* have difficulty in making an analysis.

Other sorts of problems with tone group boundaries arise from the
occurrence of pauses in speech which do not coincide with the
boundaries of units that we would like to identify as tone groups on
other criteria. Consider these examples:

Figure 3.3

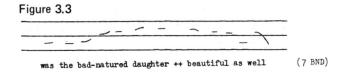

was the bad-natured daughter ++ beautiful as well   (7 BND)

The double plus here marks a fairly long pause but the overall
pitch contour appears to be carried on through this pause. It might
seem reasonable to analyse this as a single tone group with the
speaker pausing in the middle while he is selecting beautiful.
However, we also find examples where the syllable immediately
preceding the pause has considerable pitch movement on it:

Figure 3.4

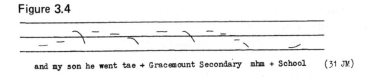

and my son he went tae + Gracemount Secondary mhm + School   (31 JM)

If we were to take account of the criteria proposed by Crystal, we would have to analyse this as four tone groups: <u>and my son</u>, <u>he went tae</u>, <u>Gracemount Secondary mhm</u>, <u>School</u>. Indeed perhaps this would be the reasonable anaylsis to make, since the speaker is having difficulty with dragging up the lexical items he wants, (a well-documented phenomenon since Goldmann-Eisler, 1958) and he therefore produces a sequence which is not absolutely coherent. He presumably experiences it as not absolutely coherent and obviously it is this same sequence which his hearer experiences. Note, however, that if we assume this is the correct analysis here we must, presumably, also analyse Figure 3.3 as a sequence of tone groups separated by a pause, since here, also, the speaker does not, in fact, produce a fluent, absolutely coherent utterance, and the hearer does, in fact, have to cope with the discontinuity.

These two examples exemplify a methodological problem which arises constantly as we encounter the less-than-totally coherent utterances of spontaneous speech. If we accept that tone groups are realised by phonetic features which include pitch and pause phenomena, we will necessarily keep encountering what appear to be conflicting criteria. Let us summarise our position at this point. We have said that we would like to regard the tone group as the realisation of a chunk of information. If the speaker is speaking fluently, tone groups will usually have syntactic coherence, in the sense of consisting of whole constituents, and semantic coherence, in the sense that items within the tone group must be interpreted with respect to each other. (For an example of this consider the discussion on <u>last year</u> and what it modifies, above.) The hearer will then experience comfortably chunked items which must be co-interpreted. However, if the speaker is under pressure, having difficulty working out just what it is he wants to say, or having difficulty in selecting the ideal lexical item, he will often speak in spasms of the sort we exemplify in Figures 3.3 and 3.4, where syntactic and semantic coherence is interrupted by pause or pitch phenomena or both. Our phonetic transcription (the transcription based on the analyst's auditory perception) will necessarily reveal this discontinuity. In some cases the utterance may adhere very closely to, say, the pitch contour structure of a tone group, as in Figure 3.3, or deviate considerably from it, as in Figure 3.4. If we want to be able to talk about 'deviance' in this sense, we shall have to try to say what we mean by it.

In describing the vagaries of performance in spontaneous speech we have a peculiar problem in describing 'deviance' in intonation which does not arise to the same extent if we look at, say, syntactic deviance or segmental deviance. When a speaker produces an utterance in the stream of speech which an analyst feels is ungrammatical, or unacceptable in context, he may relate the utterance to paradigms of system sentences (Lyons, 1968) in order to account for its deviance. Similarly if a speaker produces a deviant sequence of phonetic segments, say when he is drunk, an analyst may relate these segments to some set of standard segments of the speech community or norms for the individual. It is of course true that there are problems with these procedures, problems which are clearly common to intonation analysis as well. But the real difficulty for the intonation analyst arises not so much with techniques of relating, say, utterances to system sentences and procedures for determining whether or not an utterance is grammatical or acceptable, but in not yet having available to him the paradigm of 'system intonation'. We can produce limited models, as we have tried to do in Chapter 2, but the relationship of the 'ideal' contour generated by such a model and what we encounter in speech seems particularly remote. The problem with intonation in the stream of speech is, as we have shown in Chapter 2, that it is susceptible to so many different variables, all of which may influence its realisation. Thus, when a speaker gets stuck in the stream of speech and produces a spasmodic string of phrases, we have no obvious paradigms to relate this incoherent sequence to. In some cases, it is true, the speaker may be so dissatisfied with what he has produced that he goes right back to the beginning of such a sequence and produces it again, this time fluently. Without a doubt such examples constitute a valuable check on the correctness of the structures which a model predicts, because in such cases the speaker gives the impression of being consciously aware that he has got right what he was trying to produce. (We do not suggest that the speaker intends to 'correct' the intonation of his utterance rather than any other aspect of it. On the contrary, he is trying to get all aspects of it right.) Unfortunately in our data such complete self-corrections are rare. It is clear though, that there is a sense in which a speaker knows that he has produced a deviant utterance and there is a threshold level beyond which the amount of deviance is intolerable and he corrects the utterance. What we need to specify is the status of the relationship between the first incoherent sequence and the corrected version. We would like to propose that the corrected tone group structure has a special status very like that of a 'system sentence'. The tone groups which remain uncorrected in the stream of speech, that is, very nearly all of them, would then bear a varying relationship to the system tone group. Some are sufficiently like the model paradigm to be in a very close relationship with it as in Figure 3.3 above. Others are so deviant from this model paradigm that the relationship is much more difficult to specify, as is the case with Figure 3.4.

In our view, then, the tone group may be regarded as an abstract theoretical unit* which may be brought into relation with some of the pitch units that we encounter in the stream of speech. With others the relationship is far more difficult to specify. It does not seem to us practicable or profitable to argue about which bits in the problem examples which we cited are or are not tone groups. Rather, we take the view that we need a model which will predict the chunking of speech into units, taking into account constituent-structure (for a *pro tem.* model see Crystal, 1975) and topic-structure (see Dahl, 1976), a model which at this point in time we are far from being able to conceive adequately. With the advent of such a model, we could begin to attempt to bring the incoherent structures we encounter in spontaneous speech into relationship with it and talk meaningfully in terms of deviance from it. Until that time we simply have to say that there are many stretches of spontaneous speech which we are unable to segment into units which can be brought into relation with tone groups.

The problems we mention here are only representative of a large group of problems which we shall discuss in detail later in this chapter and in Chapter 5. They arise both from the difficulty of assigning tone group boundaries in a principled way and from identifying the location of tonics. Since we encounter constant difficulty in identifying tone groups in spontaneous speech, rather than talk in terms of abstract 'system' tone groups and deviance from them, we offer here an analysis which depends, not on the identification of tone groups (and hence of unique tonic within each tone group) but on a phonetically defined unit, the *pause-defined* unit. In some cases it will be relatively easy to perceive structures that we can relate to tone group structures within pause-defined units. However, as we shall argue, the principal pointer to these structures is usually syntactic rather than intonational. As we proceed with our description of spontaneous speech we will continually revert to the question of

*As we understand it, this view is inconsistent with Halliday's notion of 'tone group' which must relate to the utterance the speaker actually produces. As we have shown, and will continue to show, we are unable to apply this view of tone group analysis to non-fluent speech.

the potentiality for a principled tone group analysis of the data that
we are examining.

3.2. Pause-defined Units

In the task of reading texts aloud, readers usually produce fluent and
coherent chunks of speech, readily relatable to coherent syntactic/
semantic structures, which is hardly surprising since the reader is not
confronted by most of the planning decisions that a speaker speaking
in the here and now and interacting with an interlocutor is confronted
with (see Brown, 1978 for an extended discussion of this). In
producing spontaneous speech the speaker has to decide on a topic,
select the 'staging' procedures for presenting his topic (see discussion
in Grimes, 1975), determine what he must introduce as new and what
he can take as given, sort out the appropriate syntactic structures,
select lexical items, check that his listener is following what he is saying
and agreeing with it, make it clear that he wishes to continue with or
to give away his turn, quite apart from speaking. In spontaneous
speech, especially of a quite unrehearsed kind, where a speaker is more
or less painfully working out what he wants to say as he goes along,
many speakers will produce non-fluent speech. In this non-fluent
speech, many structural markers which can be relied on in texts read
aloud or fluent (partly rehearsed) public speech, disappear or fail to
co-occur with other signals which, in read texts, they regularly occur
with. Thus in read texts a syntactic boundary usually coincides with
an intonation boundary and often coincides with a pause. In non-
fluent spontaneous speech it is very common to find these boundaries
not coinciding. This may occur for many reasons — because the speaker
is having planning difficulties, because he thinks his interlocutor may
jump in and take away his turn, because he wants to create a special
effect.

The one reliable signal that we observe in spontaneous speech is
pause. This can be relied on to occur frequently, we can readily
identify it instrumentally, and instrumental readings relate very closely
to perceived pause. In the following sections we first describe our
methodological techniques, then we examine the structure of pause-
defined units in texts read aloud, then we go on to compare and
contrast the structures that we identify by these techniques in read
texts, with those that we identify in spontaneous, non-fluent speech.

3.2.i   Techniques of Analysis

Before discussing in detail how we identify these phonetic units we
must discuss the status of our techniques. We appeal to two types of
analysis, auditory and acoustic. The dangers of relying on auditory
analysis alone are well known (and documented in, for instance,
Lieberman, 1965). The analysis of a stretch of speech may vary from
person to person and the same investigator may make a somewhat
different analysis of the same data on different occasions. However,
it is clear that relying on instrumental analysis alone will also prove
inadequate since instruments do not hear like humans, a point which
Daneš (1960) states clearly: 'Granting that instruments are more
accurate and sensitive than the human ear, it is also evident that
instrumental records and their interpretations in terms of physical
acoustics do not give us a true picture of the way in which the
speakers hear and understand (evaluate) their own language . . .
The significance and function of the various waves, formants, etc . . .
must first be discovered, if only in outline, by an auditory analysis
[sic] of spoken language.'

Clearly at least two kinds of auditory analysis are possible – naive
analysis by native speakers untrained in phonetics and trained analysis
by professional phoneticians. The naive listener can be asked to listen
to a stretch of speech and divide it up into chunks where he thinks
the speaker intended a division. The resultant chunking has no special
theoretical status and cannot be directly correlated with intonation
units, syntactic units or semantic units – none the less judgements by
naive subjects show us that speakers with no formal training can
divide a speech signal into units. If it can then be established that
such 'perceptual' units coincide with formal units established with
reference to independent criteria, this provides valuable ancillary
evidence.

It is clear that units identifiable by trained phoneticians will have a
different sort of status, not only because the phonetician is trained to
listen to a variety of cues but also because he necessarily listens to his
data having regard to the theoretical framework he is working within.
So he thinks 'this must be a unit because there is a main point of
prominence in it – some loudness at the end of it – there is a drop in
pitch level at the end of this stretch – it is bounded by pauses –
there is a sharp change in pitch direction at the beginning of this bit',
and so on. He tries to think only in terms of phonetic parameters
(but the difficulties of this are well known, see again discussion in

Lieberman, 1967). So, given an utterance which he transcribes like this:

Figure 3.5

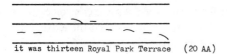

it was thirteen Royal Park Terrace   (20 AA)

he hears thirteen as salient because the pitch is highest here, and it
appears to be said louder than the rest of this sequence, whereas Royal
Park Terrace is spoken on descending pitch which returns to the
speaker's base-line and, in descending, grows perceptually less loud.
It appears to him possible to justify identifying this as a unit of
utterance in terms both of its overall pitch shape and its overall soft-
loud-soft shape. On the other hand with a sequence which he
transcribes like this:

Figure 3.6

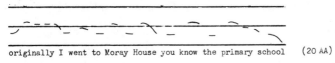

originally I went to Moray House you know the primary school   (20 AA)

the substantial change in pitch direction after the fall on House, as the
low you is pulled up sharply to the high of know, suggests to him a
probable break between two units.

In the research which provides the evidence for this study we have
relied mainly on analysis by trained phoneticians. The initial
orthographic transcription of everything said on the tape was made by
a secretary who typed the sequence of orthographic words on to sheets
of paper organised into staves. Each of the two analysts (Karen Currie
and Joanne Kenworthy) listened independently to the tape and
transcribed the pitch and pause phenomena that they perceived on to
the stave. These independent transcriptions were then compared and,
where they differed, an attempt to reach an agreed solution was made.
In some particularly recalcitrant areas, appeal was made to other local
phoneticians and to the instrumental resources of the laboratory.
Some of these cruces were later used in the experiments described in
Chapter 5.

The stave on which these impressionistic transcriptions were made
consisted of three lines. The theoretical status of this stave was unclear

but to have such a thing seemed to conform with British traditional presentation of intonation patterns (see Jones, 1962; Gimson, 1962; O'Connor and Arnold, 1959). There appears to be a general assumption that the top line represents the top of the speaker's normal voice range and the bottom line the bottom of the speaker's voice range. It very soon became clear in our transcription that the extremes of the stave were rarely used. However, some stressed syllables approximated quite closely to the top line and some even hit it. It turned out that these generally arose in turn-initial or topic-initial contexts, or under conditions of contrast or emphasis. The lowest line of the stave was used even more rarely, usually to mark a speaker's final comment on some topic. The middle line of the stave was necessary to distinguish between those syllables which were below it (usually unstressed) and those syllables which were above it (usually stressed). This stave was used for all the impressionistic transcription of the data. Note, however, that it relates in a slightly odd way to the model proposed in Figure 2.11. None of the lines in the three line stave is deemed to represent a primary theoretical level. The relationship between the two views of analysis may be represented like this:

Figure 3.7

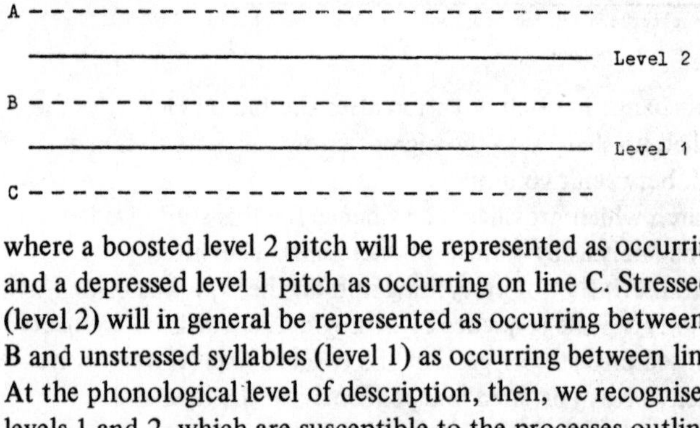

A —

——————————————————————————————— Level 2

B —

——————————————————————————————— Level 1

C —

where a boosted level 2 pitch will be represented as occurring on line A and a depressed level 1 pitch as occurring on line C. Stressed syllables (level 2) will in general be represented as occurring between lines A and B and unstressed syllables (level 1) as occurring between lines B and C. At the phonological level of description, then, we recognise two levels, levels 1 and 2, which are susceptible to the processes outlined in 2.7. and yield a phonetic realisation which may be represented on a multi-level stave. The number of levels on the phonetic stave has no theoretical implications and is determined simply by methodological convenience. (Coleman, 1914 used a five-line musical stave; Gimson, 1962 used a simple 2-line 'tube'. We prefer to work with a 3-line stave.) Corresponding to each syllable of the orthographic transcription, a line was drawn on the stave to represent the perceived pitch. If the pitch appeared to be moving the line would represent the direction of movement. The length of the line also indicates relative duration, so a syllable perceived as longer will be represented by a longer line than a syllable perceived as being shorter. Pauses are represented by + in the orthographic transcription. Where the pause is extended a ++ is used to mark this extension. A typical impressionistic transcription looks like this:

Figure 3.8

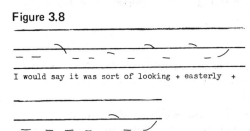

We did not use a special convention to represent stress, since stressed syllables are regularly marked in the impressionistic transcription either by being higher in pitch or by being longer or by considerable pitch movement.

Whereas instrumental analysis has the advantage of consistency, in that the instrument will yield the same reading for a given parameter each time the same data is submitted to it, there are disadvantages associated with this method of analysis quite apart from the crucial one already mentioned (that instruments do not listen like speakers of a language). The most obvious disadvantages are that instrumental evidence has to be interpreted by fallible human experimenters, instruments often need adjustment to cope with different voice-types so that not all readings are strictly comparable, instruments are variably sensitive to different parameters in different voice-types. In spite of the problems associated with instrumental investigation, we do rely on instrumental readings as confirmatory evidence for our auditory analysis in identifying units of intonation and, indeed, in the following section most of our findings are presented in terms of instrumental analysis, though originally analysed auditorily.

3.2.ii Characteristics of Pause-defined Units

We began looking at pause-defined units in the speech that subjects produced reading a short story aloud. This data had the advantage of allowing us to compare directly the 'chunking' of the same message, and the speakers were, of course, constrained in their choice of organisation into intonation units by the punctuation of the written passage. Six informants read the text — 3 males and 3 females, with one male and one female in the 20-30 age group, one female in the 30-40 age-group, one male and one female in the 40-50 age-group and one male over 50. All the informants are ESE speakers, from the south of Edinburgh. This is the short story.

The Witch's Daughter

In the midst of a range of wild mountains was a small straw hut, where an old man lived with his three sons. Every day the father went out to look for fuel.

Once he met in the wood an aged widow in white clothes, who was seated on a square stone playing chess. Since the old man was a keen player himself, he asked the woman, 'may I watch the game?' She replied, 'do you want to play with me?' 'Certainly,' said the old man. When the widow asked for what stakes they should play, he suggested playing for his wood. But the old woman said, 'No, we can't play for wood, because I don't have any wood. How many children have you, though?' 'Three sons,' was his answer. 'Three sons? That is perfect. I have three daughters. If you win, I will send them as brides for your three sons; but if I win, you must send me your sons as sons-in-law.' The old man stroked his beard for a while, but finally gave his assent.

He lost each of the games they played, and when the widow got up to leave she said, pointing down into a dark valley, 'there is my house. Tomorrow send me your eldest son, three days later the second, and again after three days the youngest.' She then departed, and the old man went home, without collecting any more wood, to tell his sons what had happened. How pleased they were when they heard it!

The next day he sent the eldest son; three days later, the second; and on the sixth day he sent the youngest.

The following information was obtained from a mingograph printout of the analysis of pitch by the Frøkjaer-Jensen Transpitch-meter and of intensity by the Frøkjaer-Jensen Intensity Meter:

Figure 3.9

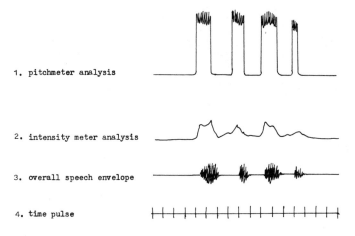

1. pitchmeter analysis

2. intensity meter analysis

3. overall speech envelope

4. time pulse

We measured the fundamental frequency (Fo) of each pitch movement in cycles per second (cps) and drew graphs representing the pitch movement from these figures. Then from the characteristics of the intensity wave form and the form of the overall speech envelope we assigned Fo measurements to each word in the text. (Where there was considerable movement on one word we measured the movement and assigned two sets of figures, one showing the beginning point and one the end point. Movement on one word is shown therefore by two hyphenated sets of figures below the word. Where figures for two adjacent words show a higher value for the first than for the second, the first word should be understood as falling towards the pitch of the second word (see discussion in 2.7.vi). That is to say, in these cases we do not give two sets of figures for the word uttered on a fall. Occasionally no separate measurement is given for a grammatical item (usually the). In this case the item is held to lie between the two measurements bounding it. We always checked this 'automatic' assignment auditorily.*

The readings achieved by this method, represented in Figure 3.10 were then converted to a graph representation in Figure 3.11.

*Amplitude peaks corresponded very regularly with Fo peaks, therefore amplitude is not discussed as a separate parameter.

Figure 3.10

Every	day	the	father	went	out	to	look	for	fuel
200–225–210			210		160		180–160		200–160
200–250–225			225–180		200–170		160		200–160
230–275–250			300–200		210–190		170	200	245–160
140	140–100		130–110		120		110–120–115		130– 95
130–150–100			140–110		110		135–115		145–110
160–150	175–135		140		120		110–140		160–120

Figure 3.11

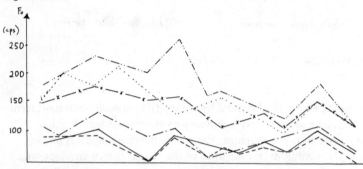

In Figure 3.10 the readings for each speaker are represented along each line. In Figure 3.11 all the graphs for each speaker are placed on a calibrated table. The value of this presentation is that it permits a quick assessment of the points of similarity and difference between the readings of individuals, at least in terms of the peaks and troughs of the intonation contour. Similar information, but this time showing one speaker's reading of different sentences in the text, adjusted so that stressed syllables coincide, appears in Figure 3.12.

We first paid attention to *pause* since this is particularly easy to identify when the pitchmeter reading, the intensity reading and the voice signal all return to their respective base-lines, indicating silence as illustrated in Figure 3.13.

Figure 3.12

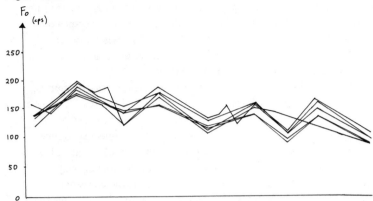

Figure 3.13 (showing a pause of 0.9 secs.)

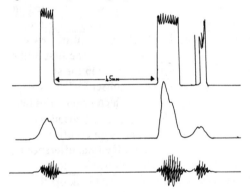

The measurements derived from this operation were then written into the text for each speaker's rendering as shown in Figure 3.14.

Figure 3.14

an aged widow	in white clothes
20	17
12	20
28	20
18	24
	37
	44

By comparing pause readings between speakers we were able to identify points in the text where all speakers paused, and to measure those, as well as points in the text where only one or two speakers paused. Any sequence bounded by substantial pauses (between 0.6 and 0.8 secs.) was later subjected to an analysis of the internal relationship holding between its Fo readings.

The patterning of pause length in the text readings corresponds, hardly surprisingly, to the semantic structuring of the text. Thus the longest pause for most subjects occurs after The old man stroked his beard for a while but finally gave his assent. (All subjects produce pauses of well over one second here.) An almost equal length of pause precedes this sentence. Note that the sentence occurs half-way through the text, and separates the setting-up of the chess-playing from what happens as a result of the chess-playing. It expresses the outcome of the conversation and is separated off from what follows by the visual blank of paragraph division. Other long pauses of over a second's duration occur for some speakers after . . . who was seated on a square stone playing chess, again, after three days, the youngest and how pleased they were when they heard it. From the point of view of narrative sequence these pauses do not seem surprising. The first of the three introduces what has to be an eventful encounter in the story. We have been told that the old man went out to collect fuel every day but then we have a new orthographic paragraph which begins with his meeting this mysterious widow. The readers, having read ahead, as efficient readers do, must be aware that this is to be an eventful confrontation. The second of this series is, again, the final utterance in a conversation of the sort which preceded The old man stroked his beard for a while . . . It appears to be conventional to block off the here and now of direct speech from the there and then of the narrative. The third of this series is another example of a paragraph-final-pause which again marks a break in the narrative time-sequence. Pauses here clearly coincide with major semantic breaks in the conceptual structure of the narrative. We may note here a point we shall return to later in this chapter, which is that the organisational blocking of speech paragraphs (as manifested by pauses and, as we shall see, also by pitch patterning) produces shorter units, even in written texts read aloud, than typical orthographic paragraphs. We shall find this to be even more strikingly the case in spontaneous speech. In this text reading at least three of the six readers paused for more than a second after:

. . . where an old man lived with his three sons

Every day the father went out to look for fuel (all readers)
. . . who was seated on a square stone playing chess
'Certainly,' said the old man
How many children have you though?
. . . you must send me your sons as sons-in-law
. . . but finally gave his assent (all readers)
. . . and again after three days the youngest
How pleased they were when they heard it (all readers)

We shall call these long pauses 'topic pauses', indicating the reader's
organisation of the text into speech paragraphs.

Other, shorter pauses of between 0.4 and 0.8 seconds also occur in
these readings, demarcating shorter units of speech. Once again
comparisons were made between the various readers to see where
pauses co-occurred. The Fo patterns in terms of peaks and troughs
of units demarcated by such short pauses were compared (i) between
different speakers reading the same part of the text (see Figures 3.15
and 3.16) and (ii) between different units of the text bounded by
short pauses produced by one speaker (see Figure 3.17). Our hypothesis
was that these units, arising in a style of speech where the speaker
simply had to utter pre-formed syntactic-semantic structures, would
yield consistent internal pitch patterns. Reference to Figures 3.15,
3.16 and 3.17 will make it clear that there are regularly recurring
pitch patterns. The rest of this chapter will be devoted to examining
these patterns, first in the text readings and then in spontaneous speech.

3.3. Contours in the Text Readings

3.3.i   The Base-line

Using the pause criteria discussed in the previous section, we isolated
266 contours in the six readings, approximately 44 contours per text.
Of these contours 40 contained a single peak of prominence, 144
contained two peaks and 82 contained three or four peaks. A peak of
prominence is defined as a peak from which a downward movement
falls, on both sides if it is medial in a contour. Figure 3.18 shows a
typical two-peaked contour where X and Y mark the peaks of
prominence and a, p and b the base-line points from which the peaks
arise.

Figure 3.15: Initial Clauses (22 BS)

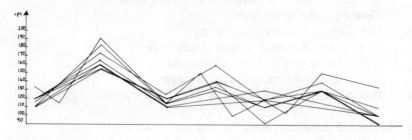

Figure 3.16: Final Clauses (22 BS)

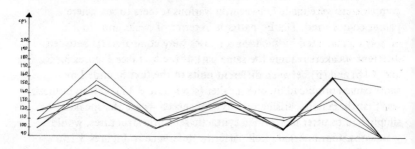

Figure 3.17

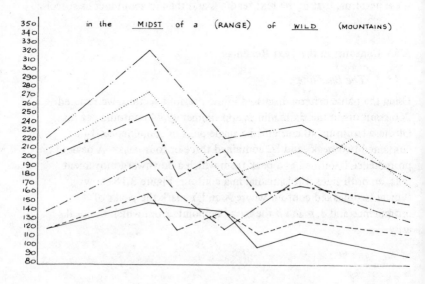

Figure 3.18

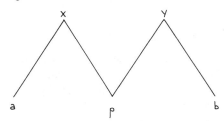

The three points *a, p* and *b* form a very consistent base-line within each contour unit, for the majority of contours, with only a narrow range of variation, around 20-30 cps. Thus for reader 11 MR, out of a total of 44 units each of which has a beginning point *a* and an end-point *b*, 27 out of 44 beginning points lie between 150 and 180 cps and 36 out of 44 end-points lie between 140 and 160 cps. 31 of the units produced by this speaker contain central base-line pivot points *p* and all 31 pivot points lie between 150 and 160 cps. So for speaker 11 MR we can state that the majority of her *a*s, *p*s and *b*s will lie between 140 and 180 cps. Her base-line then varies over 40 cps, the initial point having the widest variation, the pivot point the narrowest variation and the end-point having the lowest pitch range. How do we account for this range of variation?

The starting point *a* can jump as much as 100 cps when, following a topic pause, the speaker begins a new topic or sub-topic. Thus, whereas most of speaker 11 MR's *a*s lie between 150 and 180 cps, her starting point for the sentence The old man stroked his beard for a while is 270 cps. She has several other topic switches which yield frequencies of between 200 and 220 cps for the base-line onset *a*.

The end-point of a unit is raised (i) in places in the text where the syntax and semantics do not signal 'more to come' but, none the less, there is more to come and (ii) during the reading of direct speech.

The pivot points are the most stable of the base-line points and most of the deviation from them occurs during reading of direct speech. Thus speaker 16 LK, whose normal base-line range is between 170 and 200 cps, produces a pivot point of 245 cps in How many children have you though? The whole contour here is raised high in the pitch range of speaker 16 LK, a feature common to questions which ask the hearer for information which the listener cannot possibly know the answer to. The wholesale raising of the total contour for this question in direct speech must account for this only deviation from normal range for the pivot point by speaker 16 LK. In the text read by speaker 11 MR there are no deviations at all from her pivot-point range of 150 to 160 cps.

3.3.ii   *Double-peaked Contours and Related Multi-peak Contours*

There appear to be three patterns for double-peaked contours (i) where X is greater than Y, (ii) where Y is greater than X and (iii) where the two peaks are deemed to be perceptually equal. We shall begin by discussing the first of these patterns, where X is greater than Y.

This pattern occurs regularly in all six texts, in initial clause position in sentences and especially in topic-initial position following topic pauses as in:

> In the midst of a range of wild mountains . . .
> Every day the father went out . . .
> Once he met in the wood . . .
> Since the old man . . .
> The old man stroked his beard for a while . . .
> He lost each of the games . . .
> Tomorrow send me your eldest son . . .
> How pleased they were . . .
> The next day . . .
> and on the sixth day . . .

(For detailed analysis of these contours see Appendix A.)

Each of these units except the last is initial in a sentence and more clauses follow within this sentence. In most cases the initial raised peak X is preceded by a raised base-line initial *a*. In the last case it is the very last clause of the text which is realised in this way, where <u>sixth</u> is cumulatively contrasted with <u>next</u> and <u>three days later</u>. Individual speakers also produce this contour at other points in the reading but without the same total agreement which occurs in the clauses listed above.

We relate to the contour structure X is greater than Y, other structures where the initial peak is greater than those which follow, i.e. where X is greater than Y_1 and Y_2 (and Y_3).

There is a marked similarity of distribution between contours where X is greater than Y and those where X is greater than Y_1 and Y_2 — indeed in many cases one reader selects the first of these and another selects the second in reading the same clause. Like the double-peaked contour, this multi-peaked contour occurs in initial structures. We therefore propose to identify both these initial height double-peaked and multi-peaked structures as 'initial-peaked contours'.

The second type of contour structure that we recognise is where the final peak Y is greater than the preceding peak X. This contour has a much wider range of environments than the initial-peaked contour. It can occur in any of the following environments:

1. Where an item near the end of the contour is contrasted.
2. In a direct question.
3. In a sentence-final clause.

Examples of 1. are because I don't have ANY wood, I have three DAUGHTERS and three days later the SECOND, of 2. are Do you want to play with me? and How many children have you though? and of 3. are where an old man lived with his three sons, who was seated on a square stone playing chess and to tell his sons what had happened.

$X < Y$ contours also arise where one or more preceding peaks are less prominent than the final peak (i.e. $X_1, (X_2) (X_3) < Y$) – there are only eleven examples of these in the total 266 contours and, of these, nine occur where there is a contrasted word near the end of the clause. An example of this type is shown in Figure 3.19 where the numbers represent frequency in cps.

Figure 3.19

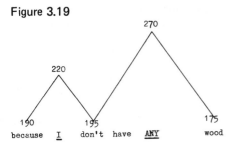

In this example, ANY is the contrasted element and is realised by a final peak which is more than 60 cps greater than the preceding peaks. The remaining nine contrastive clauses all yield a similar pattern. The two other examples of this pattern arise on final clauses. It will be clear that, once again, the distribution of these multi-peaked contours is expressible in the same terms as those suggested for double-peaked contours. We therefore treat all types of final-peaked contours as a single category.

There are obviously problems associated with our third category of contours — those in which we claim that peak X is perceptually equal to peak Y. There are clearly many features which operate to influence pitch perception other than simple fundamental frequency (see discussion in 2.7.vi), in particular the pitch environment in which a particular peak occurs. We did attempt some independent validation of our judgement of equality of pitch prominence and long-suffering phonetician colleagues were asked to identify, from a series of contours presented to them, any contours which contained two equally prominent peaks of pitch. They were asked to listen in particular for phonetic rather than semantic cues and to concentrate on pitch height and amount of pitch movement. Of those contours which we wished to identify as containing equal peaks, 80 per cent were judged by at least one judge to have equal pitch height and movement and in the remaining contours the judges made inconsistent judgements — some holding that the first peak was more prominent and the rest that the second was. This suggests to us that at least any difference in perceptual prominence was not clearly marked. The difficulty of controlling investigations using natural speech in this area can hardly be overemphasised. For the moment we retain the characterisation of this set of contours as 'equal-peaked' contours. We identified 64 contours out of the total 266 as equal-peaked.

Here are some examples of contours found in the text readings where two peaks of prominence rose to the same height in cps and descended to the same base-line:

	X	Y	a X	p	Y b
16 LK	without collecting any more wood		170-180	160	180-160
	X Y				
16 LK	three sons		250 —	210	250-210
	X	Y			
11 MR	pointing down into a dark valley		165	160	165-160
	X_1	X_2	X_1	X_2	
11 MR	you must send me your sons as		160-265-160	260 160	260-160
	Y				
	sons-in-law				

Other examples of equal-peaked contours are to be found in Appendix A. Some of these examples include sequences where a lesser peak intervenes between the two equal peaks as shown in Figure 3.20.

Figure 3.20

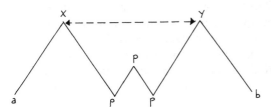

Examples of this type of contour follow, where the item underlined discontinuously is the intervening peak or peaks.

		a	X	p	P	p	Y	b
14 WF	three sons that is perfect	210-120	340 –	180	190	170	290-140	
11 MR	every day the father went out to look for fuel		200	225	160	18C	160	200-160
16 LK	where an old man lived with his three sons	200 190	210	160		190	170	225-180
11 MR	who was seated on a square stone playing chess	170 150	210	160	180-160	180-155	225-180	

The distribution of the qual-peaked contour is in any medial position, following an initial clause and preceding a final one, where there is no contrasted or specially emphasised item occurring in the clause.

3.4. Analysis and Model

It must be clear that there is a straightforward relationship between the contours that we have isolated in analysing the readings of the text and the model proposed in 2.7. We find here a neutral contour, which contains equal peaks of prominence and is distributed in non-initial and non-final position. We find an initial contour which is marked by raising the first peak (and, by tonal sandhi, any preceding unstressed syllables) and a final contour which is marked by maximum height or movement on the final peak. Contrast is also marked by an excursion to high.

This, of course, still leaves all sorts of problems. The units we are presented with in texts read aloud are organised into clear clause structures and the conventions of punctuation tend to enforce divisions at clause boundaries. Written clauses tend to be a good deal longer, and to show much more hypotactic organisation than we generally encounter in spontaneous spoken language. How far are the generalisations we have made on the basis of written texts read aloud going to carry over into the analysis of spontaneous speech? We shall consider this in 3.6.

3.5.   Contours and the Tone Group

Our methodology for identifying contours in texts read aloud is fairly straightforward and presents us with few problems of analysis. We rest initially on the identification of criterial pauses and then move to the internal analysis of the pitch pattern within units thus identified. We shall see in the next section how this methodology applies to spontaneous speech — naturally we shall expect to encounter many more problems when we are attempting to describe speech produced in an ongoing interactive context, permeated with performance variables. At this point, though, we are satisfied that the units we identify have a statable distribution, and different functions, and that there is a reasonable amount of correlation between any auditory analysis that we produce and the peak-trough analysis that we make using Fo data.

Consider the relationship between the two analyses in Figure 3.21.

Figure 3.21

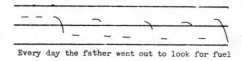

Every day the father went out to look for fuel

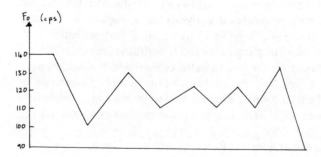

How does our pause-defined unit relate to, say, Halliday's tone group?
It must be clear that the vast majority of units that we recognise
contain two peaks of prominence. Halliday's tone group is specified in
terms of one tonic movement, though of course the stressed item
initial in the pre-tonic may constitute another peak of prominence
Clearly our peak-initial contours and double-peaked contours must
constitute a problem for a Hallidaian analysis, though the final-peaked
contours could be accommodated if we assume the initial peak(s) is
indeed merely prominent in the pre-tonic. Another possible analysis
would be to suggest that every pause-defined unit containing two peaks
is to be analysed as two tone groups. This naturally occurred to us and,
in order to see whether this might still be the most insightful analysis
and agree with the intuitions of judges trained in phonetics, we
instituted the long series of experiments that we describe in Chapter 5.
In the light of the results of those experiments, and also because we
could not find any consistent phonetic criteria which would permit us
to make divisions within the pause-defined units that we identified, we
have not attempted a conventional 'tone group' analysis. Note that one
outcome of this decision is that we are able to describe contour types
with distinct privilege of distribution.

3.6. Pause-defined Units in ESE Spontaneous Speech

We faced a choice at this point in our description. The techniques of
instrumental analysis which were performed on the text readings, and
the auditory analysis which then relates the instrumental data to the
words of the text, are extremely time-consuming. This meant we
could either examine very short stretches from a number of different
speakers or investigate a more extended text spoken by one speaker.
We have chosen to deal with only one speaker since only one base-line
then has to be established and the characteristic patterns of this
speaker becomes familiar. It follows that we can make no very general
claims on the basis of this one speaker. However we should point out
that he (22 BS) was one of the readers whose speech we examined in
the last section and, in reading the text, he produced contours of the
same kind and with the same distribution as other members of the
text-reading group. He sounds to us like a typical ESE speaker. Our
assumption is that other speakers of this accent do operate the system
that we describe here.

The data which we analysed was taken from a conversation with

Karen Currie about changes in the South Side of Edinburgh where the
speaker had lived all his life. Karen has commented that he must have
seen many changes in the South Side and he replies 'tragic changes'.
She then asks him what changes he regrets most. The excerpt we discuss
here is taken from the beginning of his answer to this question. The
text of the excerpt is presented in the same way as the reading texts,
with the Fo marked under each word. Where any pause-defined unit
contains a very short pause of less than 0.2 seconds we mark it with +
(only one occurs in this excerpt), the length of other pauses is given in
the text.

ESE Spontaneous Speech (22 BS)

1. I   regret + putting the people out of   the out
    155   200   150   115   190   160 120 115 120
    of   the   South   Side   and   central   Edinburgh you
    105 105 120-110 120-105 110 120-115 120-100 105
    know   ++ 0.86
    140-100

2. I   don't   think ++ 1.8
    145   175   100

3. especially after   the war you know after the ++ 0.64
    165-115 140-110   150 110 120   150   100

4. war   when they started the ++ 0.32
    120   120   100 130-100 100

5. redevelopment   and   the ++ 1.00
    105-120-100-120   110   110

6. well   the   authority   more   or   less   made   it   that
    120   135   165-100   120   100   140   100
    everybody was   to   go   outside you   know   ++ 0.68
    125-100   100   100 100 130-95   130-100

7. the   gardens   and   houses   but ++ 0.28
    90   130-110   100   120-90   120

8. I   would   reckon   that   eighty   per cent of   the
    160   120-100 100   140   140-100 120 100
    people ++ 0.78
    120-90

9. didnae   want   to go   out   of   the   town didnae
    150-120 160   100   100   100   125   100
    want   their   gardens   they   were   quite   happy
    125-95 115   115   110   130   130

where	they	were	if	they'd	<u>built</u>	houses
100	110	120-100	125	115	125	100

<u>in</u> the town (mhm) ++ 0.82
150 105

10. <u>which</u> they're <u>doing</u> <u>now</u> after ++ 0.34
160-125 160-145 160-120 165 115-110

11. <u>about</u> eh ++ 0.86

12. (mhm) you know ++ 0.38

13. thirty years too <u>late</u> so to <u>speak</u>
145-120 125-115 140-120 150 130 80 110-95
you <u>know</u> (mhm) ++ 0.62
100 135-110

14. that's what I regret especially central
165-180-170 110 120-90 155-110 120-115
south Edinburgh ++ 0.8
115-110 115-130-85

15. em ++ 1.5

16. I would I <u>reckon</u> with <u>taking</u> the people
110 125 160 180 120 200 120
<u>out</u> they've ++ 0.36
140-120 125-120

17. they've <u>lost</u> the community ++ 0.82
125 165 110 130-140-90

18. <u>no</u> community <u>spirit</u> at <u>all</u> I <u>don't</u> think
180 130-90 110 120 180 140
you've the <u>same</u> <u>spirit</u> in the <u>new</u> housing
100 130 125 100 125 90
<u>schemes</u> ++ 0.7
110-90

19. as you <u>had</u> in the <u>old</u> eh ++ 0.6
100 110 115 90 120 100

20. (did eh. .) <u>type</u> of <u>dwellings</u> you <u>know</u> (mhm) ++ 1.8
110 100 110-100 130-100

This sort of speech, which is quite typical of much of the conversational speech that occurs in our data, obviously presents grave difficulties to the analyst. The speaker keeps re-planning what he wants to say and this has a disrupting effect on the organisation of the syntax and of the intonation.

3.6.i   *Pause-defined Units in Spontaneous Speech*

The pauses in this excerpt seem to fall into three types. The first is the long 'topic' pause which we identified in the read texts. Topic pauses occur after units 2 (1.8 seconds), 5 (1.0 seconds) and 15 (1.5 seconds). (A further 1.8 second pause follows unit 20 which precedes KC taking her turn.) The long pause after 2 occurs when the speaker has abandoned whatever he began to say in 2. In 3 he introduces a new element into the discussion, the time at which the depopulation occurred, after the war (which leads to a switch to past tense in unit 4). The long pause after 5, again leaves an abandoned structure behind it, and precedes a fresh start in 6 (introduced by well), where the speaker identifies the they of 4 as the authority, and expands on what happened just after the war, the authority . . . made it that everybody was to go outside. The long pause after 15 also follows an 0.8 second pause and em. It precedes 16 which introduces a new extension of the topic into the discussion, the loss of community spirit. It seems clear that the sequences of pausing after 14 marks a bigger conceptual break than the earlier, shorter pauses.

The second class of pauses relates very closely to the contour-marking class that we identified in the reading texts and varies between 0.6 and 0.87 seconds, with very much the same range as that of the reading texts. Once again we identify these as contour-marking pauses in our analysis.

The third set, which presents a remarkably consistent range of length, varies between 0.28 and 0.38 seconds. It is tempting to identify these as 'search pauses' where the speaker is having planning problems since four out of the five cases co-occur with incomplete syntax (4, 7, 10, 16) and the last one (12) occurs following you know within an incomplete syntactic structure (see Figure 3.22). However, there are other cases of incomplete syntax which are followed by contour pauses within the normal range (e.g. 3 and 11). It does seem to be the case with this speaker that these very short pauses are usually to be associated with syntactic discontinuity. However, for the purposes of this discussion we shall simply regard these short pauses as a sub-set of the contour pauses.

We have tended to discuss pauses as though they were associated with the preceding unit. A more reasonable approach would almost certainly be to associate them with what follows, and to suggest that the more planning a speaker has to do, for instance if he is introducing a whole new dimension into the discussion, the longer the preceding pause will be. This should also lead us to re-examine our notion of 'finality pause' in text read aloud, and suggest that such a pause simply mimics the planning pause needed in the production of spontaneous speech before a new topic or sub-topic is introduced.

3.6.ii   Contour Types Within Pause-defined Units

We are able to identify two out of the three contour types that we found in texts read aloud. (Again we ignore single-peaked contours — only unit 2 provides an example of this type.) We recognise initial-peak contours and equal-peak contours.

Figure 3.22: Pause-defined Units and Contour Types in ESE Spontaneous Speech

unit	pause length	pause type Topic	pause type Contour	contour type initial	contour type equal	incomplete syntax
1.	0.86		+	+		
2.	1.80	+				+
3.	0.64		+	+		+
4.	0.32		(+)		+	+
5.	1.00	+			+	+
6.	0.68		+	+		
7.	0.28		(+)		+	+
8.	0.78		+	+		
9.	0.82		+		+	
10.	0.34		(+)		+	+
11.	0.86		+		( )	(about eh)
12.	0.38		(+)		( )	(you know)
13.	0.62		+		+	
14.	[0.80]		+	+		
15.	[1.50]	+			( )	(em)
16.	0.36		(+)	+		+
17.	0.82		+		+	
18.	0.87		+		+	
19.	0.60		+		+	+
20.	1.80	+			+	

There are six examples of initial-peaked contours, in units 1, 3, 6, 8, 14 and 16. The first occurs in unit 1, the beginning of the speaker's turn, and peaks at 200 cps on regret, one of the two highest values recorded in this excerpt. Three occur immediately following the three topic pauses: units 3, 6 and 16. The initial peak in units 3 and 6 reach 165 cps, whereas that in 16, like that in 1, reaches 200 cps. We have already noted in the previous section that the pause preceding 16 is extra-long and forms part of a sequence of pause-filler(em)-pause, and that there seems to be a substantial shift of interest within the topic, the depopulation of Edinburgh, to a new sub-topic to do with the loss of community spirit. Four out of the six initial-peaked contours are, then, clearly related to initial structures. What of the remaining two? 8 introduces the speaker's personal point of view, his comment on what he was describing in 6-7 — I would reckon, he begins, with a high stressed I, peaking at 160 cps, followed by a run of lower peaks falling 20-30 cps from between 140 and 120 cps. We may note that he uses the same formula I would reckon to introduce the new sub-topic in 16. It seems reasonable to suggest that this does represent the introduction of a new element into the discourse at this point, even though the preceding pause is one of the shortest that we record, 0.28 seconds.* 14 appears to function as a summary of what the speaker has been saying so far. The initial peak shows the only instance in this data of a rise, rising from 165 to 180 cps, on the deictic that, which is followed by a series of lower peaks. It seems clear that this cannot properly be regarded as an instance of introducing a new semantic element into the discourse, which is what we have claimed for the units preceded by topic pause. We do not have enough relevant data to allow us to speculate profitably about whether a summary is normally introduced by a peak-initial contour. For the moment we simply state that four of the six contour-initial units are clearly associated with introducing new topical material into the discourse, one refocuses the discourse on to the speaker's own opinion and one introduces a summary statement.

We recognise ten equal-peak contours. Units 4 and 5 both show two low peaks, falling from 130 to 120 cps. They clearly form between them the conclusion of the statement the speaker begins in unit 3. (This pattern of lowered peaks on a low base-line is typical of the way this speaker tails away at the end of a sequence of units on the same topic.) Note that he abandons this line of development at the end of unit 5 despite the incomplete syntax, which appears to signal more to come. Unit 7 has two low peaks each falling 30 cps to the base-line. Unit 9 begins with a high peak on contrastive want and ends with a high peak on contrastive in. The peaks in between are all low, none reaching more than 130 cps, all falling back to the low base-line. These intermediate peaks we take to be 'pivot' peaks of the sort we discussed in Section 3. Unit 10 produces a set of equally high

---

*Pike (1945) states that pause-length interacts with the duration of the last word of the previous unit. We have not managed to establish a norm of duration for words of different classes in different contour-unit positions.

peaks, all between 160 and 165 cps, which arise out of a very
considerably raised base-line. (We shall consider this further in our
discussion of the base-line in 3.6.iv.) In 13 the initial peak on thirty
falls 25 cps from 145 cps and the second peak on late falls from
150 cps to 130 cps, with a tail away at the end. Unit 17 has two peaks,
lost falling from 165 to 110 cps, and community falling from 140 to
90 cps. 18 again has two peaks, no on 180 cps and don't on 180 cps
followed, again, by a tail away of low peaks falling from 125 cps to
a low base-line. 19 and 20 each contain two low peaks, had and old,
type and know. From the second high peak in 18, in I don't think, to
the end of the excerpt, we have a sequence of low peaks rising from a
low base-line, very like those in units 4 and 5.

   Since all the equal-peaked contours occur in a non-topic-initial
position and can clearly be seen to be, semantically and syntactically,
continuations of material introduced in peak-initial contours, we
propose to relate these initial-contour/equal-contour sequences to the
'paratonic' structure we discussed briefly in 2.3. Each paratone, we shall
say, is introduced by a peak-initial contour. It may then also optionally
contain one or more equal-peaked contours (see unit 14 for an example
of a paratone which contains no equal-peaked contour). We shall then
distinguish between major paratones, which follow topic pauses and are
characterised by very high peaks (in the speech of 22 BS by peaks at
around 200 cps) and minor paratones which follow contour pauses and
begin with lower peaks (typically for 22 BS between 160 and 180 cps).

   We find in this excerpt no examples of peak-final contours. How are
we to account for this? It might be possible to argue that unit 20
gives us an example of a peak-final contour with the peak on know. We
are reluctant to argue this, since the intensity falls away rapidly on
this item and it really seems no more perceptually salient than dwelling
(which is perceived as stressed, largely because dwell has considerable
duration). If we ignore perceptual salience and simply look at Fo
readings we have an attractive analysis in terms of our discussion of text
readings. None the less, we believe that we have none of the clear
conclusiveness which we found in the read texts in this excerpt. Perhaps
this should not surprise us. Perhaps we should not expect to find all the
markers which characterise highly structured written prose read aloud,
in the loosely structured, paratactic speech of casual, non-goal-directed
conversation, especially when it is often far from clear whether the
speaker will continue to speak or not. Thus we appear to have a potential
handover of turn at the end of unit 14. KC has been uttering increasingly
frequent mhms (9, 12 and 13) and the speaker appears to have reached

a possible conclusion. However, KC does not come in at this point and
the speaker starts again with unit 16. Our expectation is that more
highly structured speech, for example the sort of speech one meets in
lectures, will provide examples of peak-final contours. For the time
being, in this casual type of speech exemplified in our excerpt, we
recognise only peak-initial contours and equal-peak contours.

3.6.iii   *Pause-defined Units and Tone Groups*

How do the units which we attempt to identify in terms of formal
features of pause length and Fo values (which, naturally in auditory'
analysis we must express in terms of relative perceived pitch height)
relate to the conventional tone group? The discontinuity and pausing
of the first five units make it difficult to relate these to tone groups,
except in the case of unit 1 which might be analysed as one unit (tonic
on emphatic people) followed by a minor unit (you know). Several
other units — 6, 8, 13 and 14 — seem to be comfortably relatable to
sequences of two tone groups. We would like to spend a little time
looking at unit 9, which is clearly very long and which appears to
offer a structure that might well be analysed as a series of tone groups.
It would seem reasonable to suggest that didnae want to go out of the
town would constitute one group (tonic on contrastive want — let us
call this 9a), didnae want their gardens a second (9b — tonic again on
want), they were quite happy where they were a third (9c — tonic
not clearly marked, happy is rather a feeble candidate in this low-
pitched speech) and if they'd built houses in the town a fourth
(9d — tonic on contrastive in). It is perhaps significant that it is in this
part of the excerpt, where the speaker is speaking quite fluently and
without pause, that we feel most confident in attempting an analysis in
terms of tone groups. It is, however, also significant that the cues we
rely on in making such an analysis are largely syntactic, not intonational.
We have, for instance, a difficulty in determining where the boundaries
of tone groups lie if we appeal only to phonetic cues, except between
9c and 9d where Crystal's criterion of pitch-direction change seems to
indicate a boundary between were (120-100 cps) and if (125).
Between 9a and 9b we have town falling to 100 cps and didnae also on
100 cps, without any pause occurring between them and between 9b
and 9c, gardens they were runs on at 110 cps. We would, in fact, find
more dramatic pitch change criteria within some of these units; thus, in
9a, we have a sequence didnae want (150-120, 160), in 9b want their
(125-95, 115) and 9d houses in (100, 150). Clearly we do not identify
boundaries by these intonational leaps because the syntax forbids such

an interpretation. It is only by appeal to the syntax that we can tell where the boundaries are. Similarly we only identify the low-fall want in 9b and happy in 9c as tonics, rather than simply as stressed items falling to the base-line as most stressed items do, because tone group theory demands that we assign a tonic to each unit. It is this sort of consideration that led to the examination of the perceptual status of tone groups and tonics which we describe in Chapter 5.

Are there no items which we unhesitatingly identify as tonics in this data? It is certainly the case that there are many items which we hear as being either contrastive or emphatic. It is not, we find, an easy distinction to draw (see for example, Chafe's confident discussion, 1976).*

Figure 3.23 lists the items at issue here. All of them peak to 150 cps or above, except the last two, new and old, which respectively reach 125 and 120 and fall to the base-line. These two occur in the tail away just before the speaker gives up his turn. It is not at all obvious, in fact, that a contrast is involved as one hears new housing scheme. At this point it seems merely that new is the first member of a constituent the rest of which is given — however, when old turns up in unit 19 this, retrospectively, seems to bring new into contrast. In the other contrastive cases the only clearly formal instance of contrast is in in in the town which is in explicit contrast with out of the town which occurs at the beginning of unit 9. In the other cases no formal contrast is involved and not all listeners perceive contrast. For instance people in unit 1, which cumulates the height associated with a major paratone-initial contour and that associated with emphasis producing a very high peak, can be heard as contrastive, in which case it implies a contrast with, say, 'offices', 'cars', etc. (but, note, no specifiable set of items since no formal contrast is involved) or may merely be heard as emphatic, identifying the topic — 'what I'm talking about is the people'. The same sorts of arguments can be made for most of the items in Figure 3.23. Certainly we could put all the items in this set together and call them tonics since they all form perceptual peaks. However, this clearly leaves a lot of the text without tonic structure, if the items

*Coleman (1914) is to be credited with an attempt to draw a careful distinction between contrastive prominence and emphatic (affective) prominence. He suggested that contrastive prominence would regularly be realised by pitch height whereas emphatic prominence *may* be realised by pitch height but will also be realised by 'special stress, extra slowness, extra quickness, length of word, additional words *before* the intensified word to gain attention by keeping one waiting, pauses with the same object, and other devices such as repetition'. We are indebted to L.A.Iles for drawing this discussion to our attention.

in Figure 3.23 are the only tonics.

Figure 3.23: The Distribution of Contrastive and Emphatic Words in
    the Text

Unit	Contrastive	emphatic	(initial)
1.	people (190-160)		regret (200)
2.		don't (175-100)	
3.		especially (165-115)	
		war (150-110)	
6.		authority (165-100)	
8.	I (160-120)		
9.	want (160-100)		
	in (150-105)		
10.		which (160-125)	
		doing (160-120)	
		now (165-115)	
13.		late (120-150-130)	
14.		that's (165-180)	
		especially (155-110)	
16.			taking (200)
17.		lost (165-110)	
18.	no (180-130)	don't (180-140)	
19.	new (125-90)		
20.	old (120-100)		

We can find no principled basis for identifying other items as tonics. We note, moreover that more than half of the items listed in Figure 3.23 come at, or very near, the beginning of contours. (If we attempted a tone group analysis the position would be even more striking and nearly all of the tonic items would occur at the beginning of tone groups.) This is surprising when we consider the conventional given/ new structure of tone groups proposed in the literature. However, in the type of data we are describing here, where really rather little new information is introduced into the discussion and, when it is, it is introduced at a much less rapid rate than in, say, written texts, perhaps we should not be surprised to find a different pattern of information structure.

Although we cannot readily identify tonics that are non-contrastive or non-emphatic, none the less we do discern a clearly-marked ordering of 'newness' and 'givenness' for this speaker, which is marked by the pitch (in auditory terms) at which he utters a given item. Figure 3.24 shows, in Set One, lexical items which are actually repeated in the excerpt. It is clear that the items introduced for the first time are

introduced high in the speaker's pitch range (in Fo terms for this
extract, above 150 cps) whereas, when they are repeated, they appear
much lower in the speaker's range. The second set is introduced at very
much the same level as the repeated items. Can we account for this?
South and central Edinburgh have already been mentioned in the
conversation before this excerpt begins. We would, then, expect them
to be treated as given in this discussion of the depopulation of the
areas. go out(side) must relate back to putting . . . out in unit 1, and
town obviously relates back to Edinburgh. It seems reasonable, then, to
suggest that items introduced at this low level of the speaker's pitch
range are being treated by him as given. How are we to account for
the introduction of gardens and houses at this level in unit 7? It is a
commonplace to anyone who knows about town centre redevelopment
that the reasons given for moving the population out of the centre of
the town were improved amenities like gardens and the better standard
of housing to be found out on peripheral housing estates. Similarly it is
a commonplace to anyone who knows Edinburgh's particular case that
people were moved out from nineteenth-century tenement flats into
houses. The speaker is clearly expecting that KC, who has already
shown herself to be knowledgeable about old Edinburgh, will make
this connection. On the other hand, he does seem somewhat undecided
about how much he can assume. In 6 he appeared to be going to say
go out and leave it there, but he holds on to the final *t* in out,
producing a very long stop, and he then adds side — and then goes on,
almost muttering, the gardens and houses you know — making quite
explicit what he is talking about, but low-pitched as though he can
really assume this. As Figure 3.24 shows, items introduced at this
given level may drop even further in pitch, right down to the base-line
even, if they are repeated again.

Figure 3.24: The Fo Values of Recurring Lexical Items

Lexical item	1st Occurrence	2nd Occurrence	3rd Occurrence	Unit No.
Set One				
regret	200	120-90		1, 14
people	190-160	120-90	120	1, 8, 16
war	150-110	120		3, 4
want	160-100	125-95		9, 9
Set Two				
south	120-110	115-110		1, 14
central	120-115	120-115		1, 14
Edinburgh	120-110	115-130-85		1, 14
gardens	130-110	110		7, 9
houses	120-90	100	(housing) 90	7, 9, 18
go out(side)	100-130-95	100		6, 9
town	125-100	105		9, 9
community	130-140-90	130-90		17, 18
spirit	110	125-100		18, 18

Just as placing in the speaker's pitch range indicates to the hearer the new or given status which the speaker assigns to a lexical item, so placing in the pitch range differentiates between the amount of information carried by different types of non-lexical items. Thus, some grammatical items regularly turn up right on the speaker's base-line (articles, pronouns, auxiliary verbs, conjunctions (not but) and other familiar members of the traditional 'weak form' set) whereas others (logical connectors, so, but, a mixed set of clause subordinators, after, when, if as well as quite, same and the interactive markers, you know, well) appear with values very like those for lexical items treated as given. Figure 3.25 shows the frequency values for these different sets as well as for a third set, Set C, which includes unstressed syllables of stressed items and the end-points of movement on stressed monosyllables.

In general, then, we see the structure within contours as marked primarily by high peaks and, therefore, by a very consistent use of pitch range to indicate the relative importance of items in terms of information value.

3.6.iv   *The Base-line of Pause-defined Units*

We have made constant appeal in our discussion to the notion of the base-line of a unit from which peaks emerge. It was stated in our discussion of the base-line in 2.7. that it was conceived of as the level specified by the unstressed syllables within a unit. We need now to

modify that statement in the light of our discussion in the previous
section and to state that the base-line consists of unstressed syllables
from Set A and Set C in Figure 3.25 but not those from Set B.

Figure 3.25: Fo Values for Unstressed Syllables and Stressed
            Grammatical Items

	Set A	Set B	Set C
1.	I 155(200)	know 140	south — 110
	the 115, 115, 105		side — 105
	of (160)120, 105		central — 115
	and 110		Edinburgh — 100
	you 105		know — 100
2.	I 245(175)		
3.	the 110	especially 165	especially — 115
	you 110	after 140	after — 110
	the 100	after 150	after — 100
		know 120	
4.	they 100	when 120	started — 100
	the 100		
5.	and 110		re- 105
	the 110		redevelopment — 100-120
6.	the 135(165)	well 120	authority 100
	or 100	more 120	less 100
	it 100	every 125	body 100
	that 100	know 150	outside 95
	was 100		know 100
	you 95		
7.	the 90	but 120	gardens — 110
	and 100		houses — 90
8.	that 100		reckon — 100
	of (110) 120 (120)		per cent — 110
			people — 90
9.	to 100	if 125	didnae (150) 120 (160)
	of 100	quite 130	want — 95
	the 100		
	didnae 100		
	their 115		
	they 110		
	were 110		
	where 100		
	they 110		
	they'd (125) 115 (125)		

	Set A	Set B	Set C
10.		after 115	which — 125 they're — 145 doing — 120 after — 110
13.	to 80 you 100	so 130 know 135	thirty — 120 years — 115 late 120-150
14.	what 110	especially 155	regret — 90 especially — 110 central — 115 south — 110 Edinburgh (115) 130-85
16.	I 110 would 125 I 160 (180) with (180) 120 (200) they've 125		out — 120
17.	they've 125 (165) the 110		community 130 (140) 90
18.	at 110 you've 100 the 100 in 100 the 100	same 130	community — 90 schemes — 90
19.	as 100 you 110 in 90 the 90 (eh 100)		
20.	of 100 you 100	know 130	dwellings — 100 know — 100

Set A: traditional 'weak' forms
Set B: logical connectors, subordinators etc.
Set C: end-points of stressed monosyllables and unstressed syllables

It is necessary to distinguish between unstressed and stressed syllables in order to specify the base-line. Syllables perceived as stressed are underlined in the text (3.5.). Whereas there is an important correlation between Fo and the perception of an item as stressed, it is well known that other variables like relative duration, intensity, clarity of articulation and the degree of lexicalness of an item will interact with Fo. Reference to the text will show that by no means all high-frequency syllables are perceived as stressed or low-frequency syllables as unstressed. Figure 3.26 shows the distribution of stressed and unstressed syllables in terms of the Fo range of the speaker. We have discussed in 3.6.iii how it comes about that some lexical items are lowered in pitch. We now have to investigate the unstressed syllables which are raised in pitch.

Figure 3.27 shows clearly that the most dramatic raising of the base-line occurs in association with high peaks. Thus the peak-initial contours (1, 2, 6 and 16) which clearly begin initial structures all have raised base-lines at the beginning of the contour. (Note that the 'summary' peak-initial contour 14 drops its base-line values very rapidly.) In many other cases of raised base-line values the effect of pitch sandhi from an adjacent high-stressed item is clearly seen. Initial unstressed syllables (as in 2, 17) and syllables occurring between two high stressed items (as in 9 (1_50_, 120, 1_60_)) are particularly vulnerable to this. It is very striking, however, as one considers Figure 3.27, that, whereas in most contours the base-line drops quite rapidly to 100-110 cps after the initial peak no matter how elevated the onset, in the cases of units 10 and 16 the base-line remains at a relatively high level throughout the contour. In both these contours the speaker appears to be speaking in a particularly animated manner. The high peaks and raised base-line reflect this animation. No appeal to contour structure or information structure will allow us to account for this. We have to make appeal to the notion of 'affective meaning' we introduced in 2.1. and say that it is his emotional involvement with the topic which causes the speaker to raise the peaks, and hence the base-line, in these two contours, which we analyse as shifted up in key. We mentioned at the end of 3.3.i that in the text-reading by speaker 11 MR there were no deviations from her pivot point range of 150-160 cps, whereas the reading by 16 LK does produce an example of a very marked pivot point raising in How many children have you though. This raising of the base-line by 16 LK is accompanied by raised peaks, another example of shift-up. We hear this as being more animated than the surrounding utterances, revealing a clearly interpretive reading.

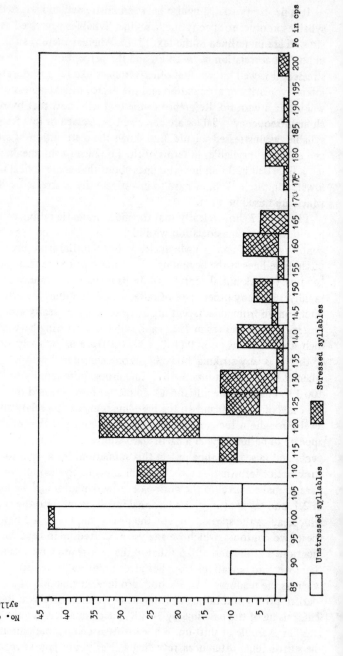

Figure 3.26: Distribution of Stressed and Unstressed Syllables in the Fo Range of 22 BS

Figure 3.27: Base-line Sequences Within Pause-defined Units

---

1. 155 (<u>200</u>) 115 (<u>160</u>) 120 115 105 105 (<u>120</u>) 110 (<u>120</u>) 105 110 115 110
    105 100
2. 145 (<u>175</u>) 100
3. (<u>165</u>) 115 (<u>140</u>) 110 110 100
4. 100 100 100
5. 105 100 110 110
6. 135 (<u>165</u>) 100 100 100 100 100 100 95 100
7. 90 110 100 90
8. 100 100 (<u>140</u>) 140 (<u>110</u>) 120 (1<u>20</u>) 90
9. (1<u>50</u>) 120 (<u>160</u>) 100 100 100 100 95 115 110 100 110 100 115 100 105
10. (<u>160</u>) 125 160-145 (<u>160</u>) 120 (<u>165</u>) 115 110
11.
12.
13. (<u>145</u>) 120 125 (<u>140</u>) 120 (1<u>50</u>) 80 100 110
14. 110 90 115 115 110 85
15.
16. 110 125 160 (<u>180</u>) 120 (<u>200</u>) 120 (<u>140</u>) 120 125-120
17. 125 (<u>165</u>) 110 130 (<u>140</u>) 90
18. 90 100 100 100 90 90
19. 100 110 90 90 100
20. 100 100 100

(Stressed items which exert an assimilatory effect of pitch sandhi are indicated in brackets)

In the reading produced by 11 MR on the other hand, with its relatively narrow pitch range and very consistent base-line, we have the impression of a very much more perfunctory reading. In general then, we suggest, a shift-up in key may signal affective meaning, particularly involvement by the speaker, if it does not occur (i) at the beginning of a new topic or (ii) in a response to a question which introduces a new topic (see 4.1.).

3.7. Conclusion

We have presented an analysis which can be applied to texts read aloud as well as to non-fluent spontaneous speech. This involves:

1. Identifying *pause-defined* units.
2. Identifying *topic pauses* and *contour pauses*. (This difference, we suggest, relates to the amount of work a speaker has to do in

producing an utterance, and should not be related to notions of
finality.)

3. Identifying *contours*. *(Peak-initial, equal-peak,* and *peak-final*
   (though note that peak-final may not occur in spontaneous
   unrehearsed speech). These contour types have distinct privilege of
   distribution with respect to topic structure.)

4. Identifying relative *pitch-level*. (Contrastive/emphatic items will be
   realised on boosted peaks, new items on high peaks, given items and
   unstressed Set B items on depressed peaks, and unstressed items
   from Sets A and C on the base-line.)

5. Identifying the height of the *base-line* relative to the speaker's norm.
   (This will be raised by tonal sandhi adjacent to boosted peaks.
   Where it is raised throughout a contour, yielding a shift-up in key,
   this appears to indicate an increased involvement with what he is
   saying on the part of the speaker.)

Naturally we do not claim that this analysis will always apply
transparently. None the less, we believe this represents an approach
which yields insights into intonation function. Even more strongly,
we believe that this is an appropriate framework of description for the
non-fluent spontaneous speech which constitutes so much of our data.
Furthermore, it enables us to draw a typological distinction between
non-fluent spontaneous speech and speech produced in text-reading
aloud: (i) with respect to the types of contour which occur in these
distinct varieties of speech and (ii) with respect to the typical
information structure of these varieties.

APPENDIX A

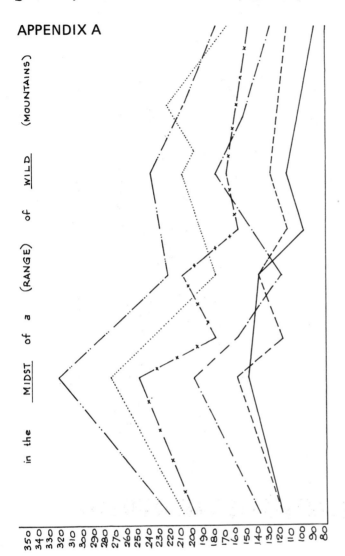

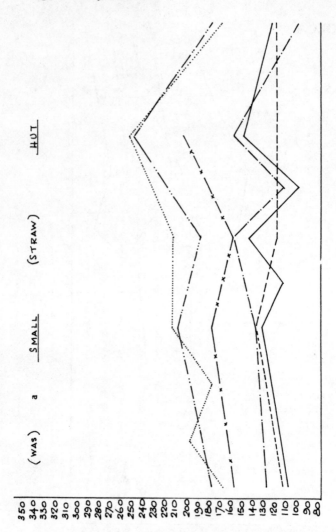

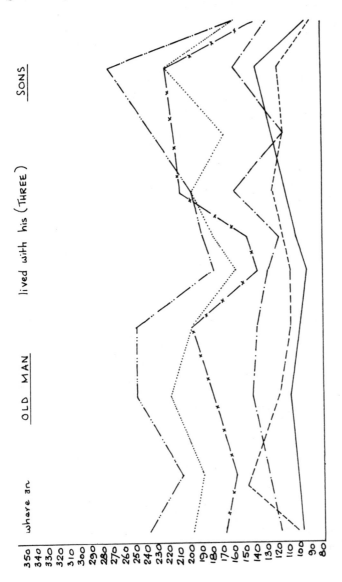

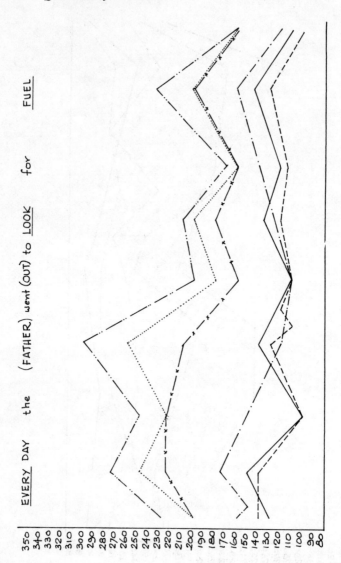

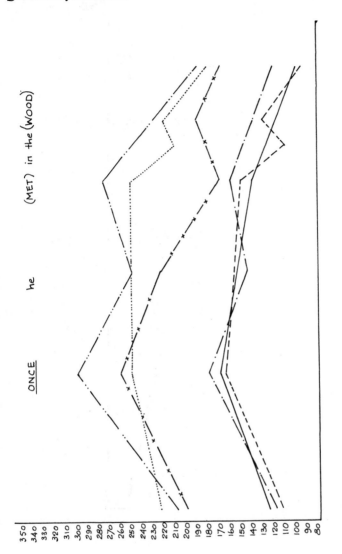

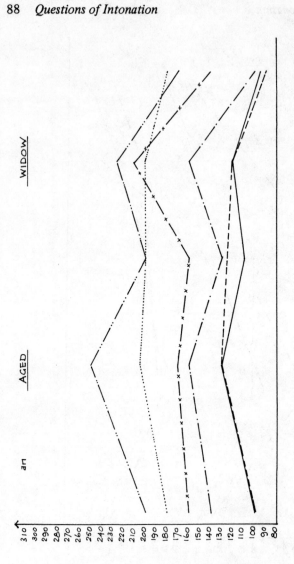

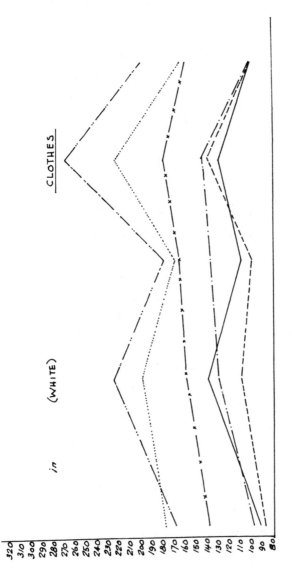

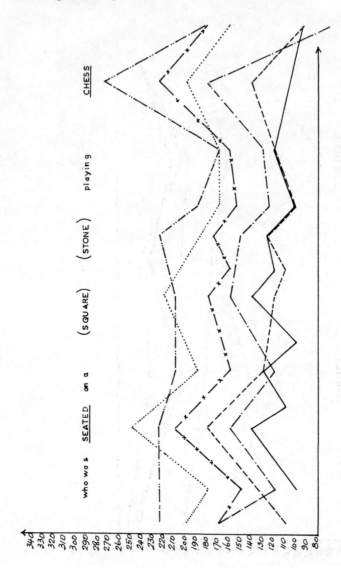

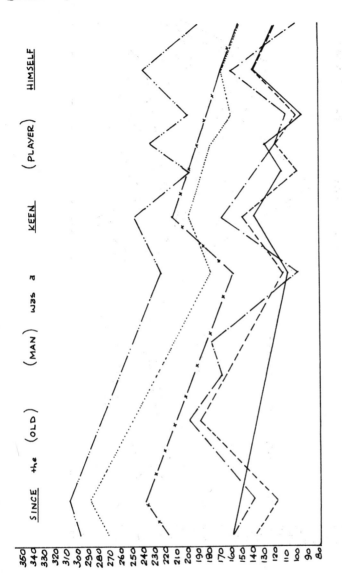

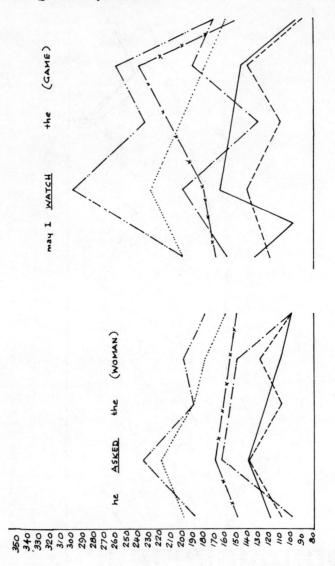

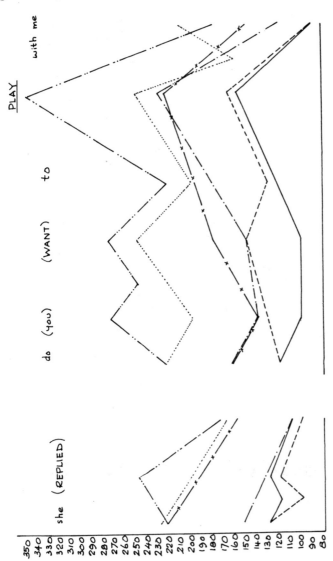

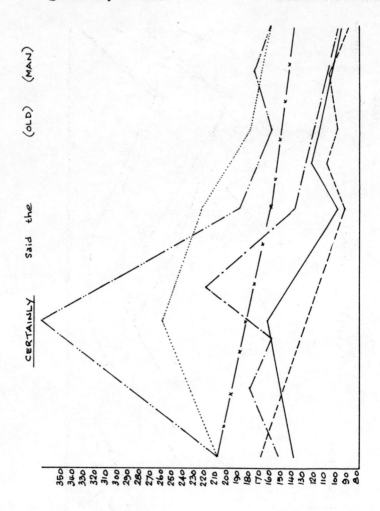

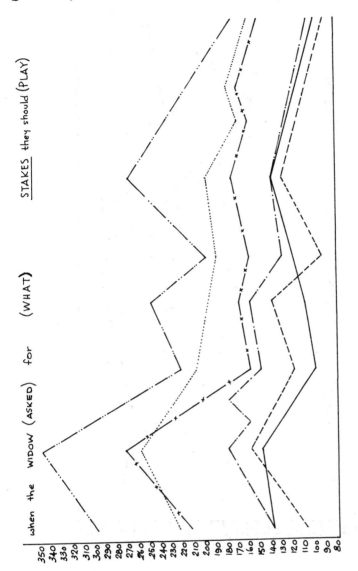

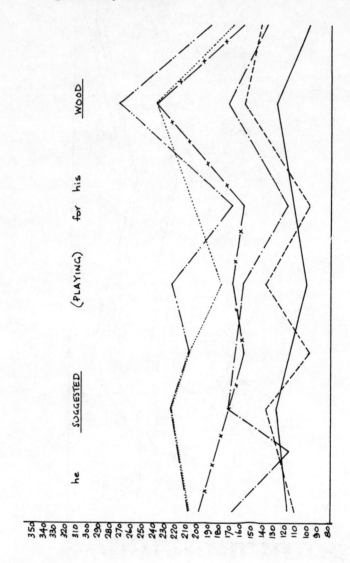

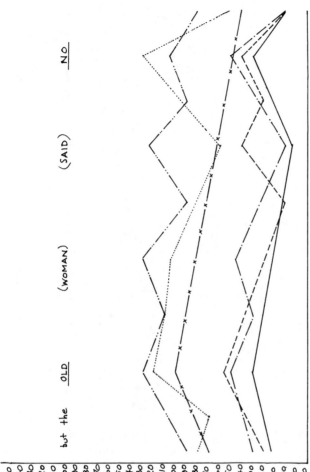

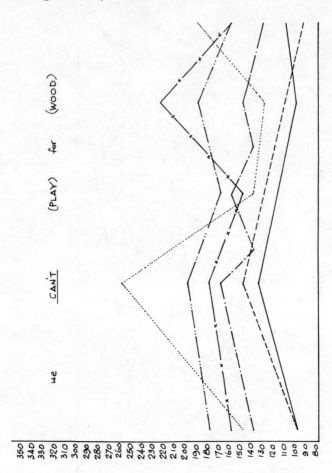

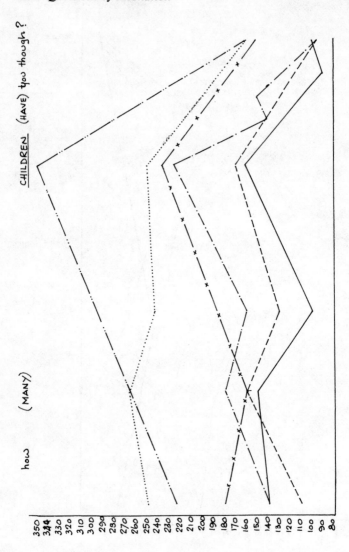

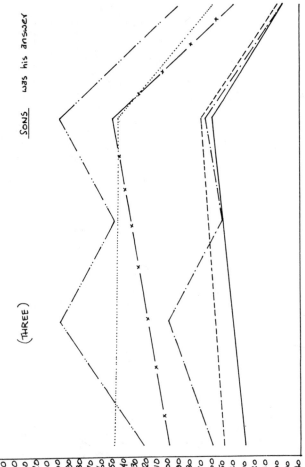

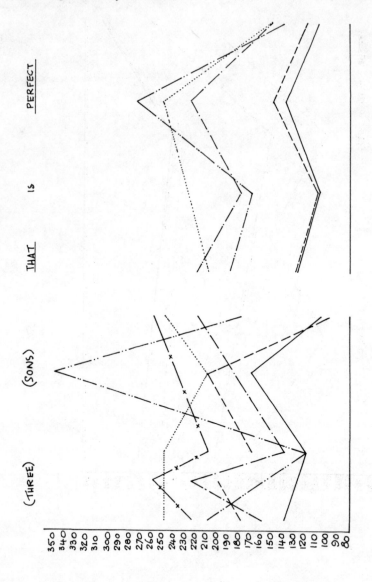

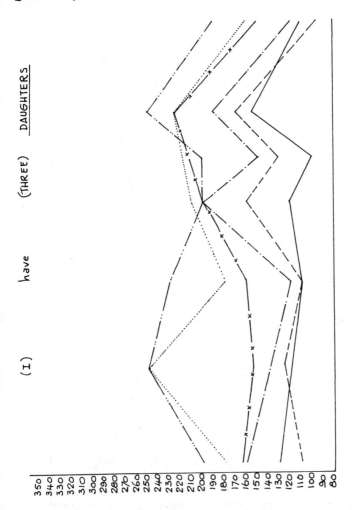

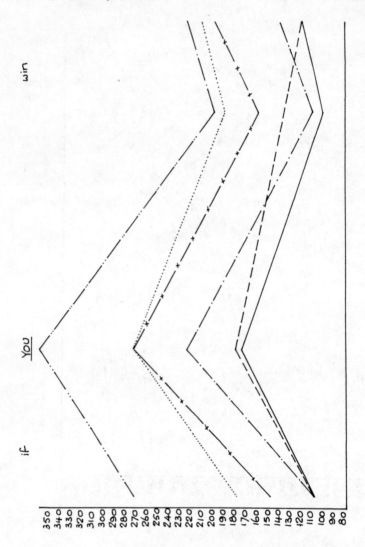

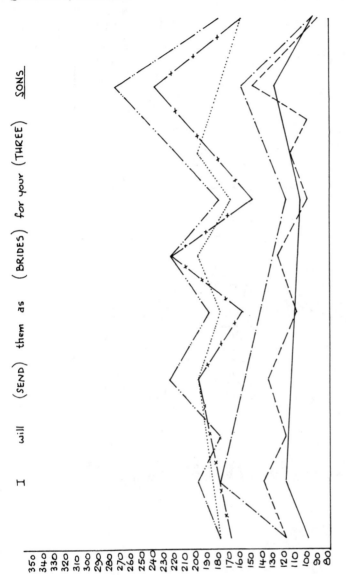

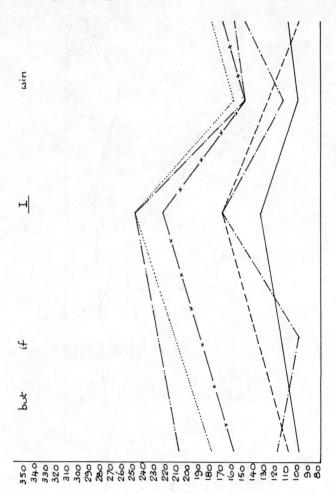

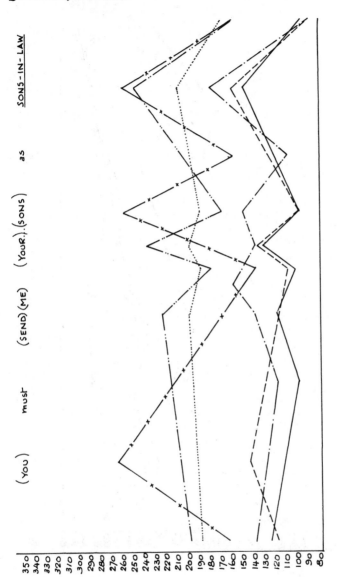

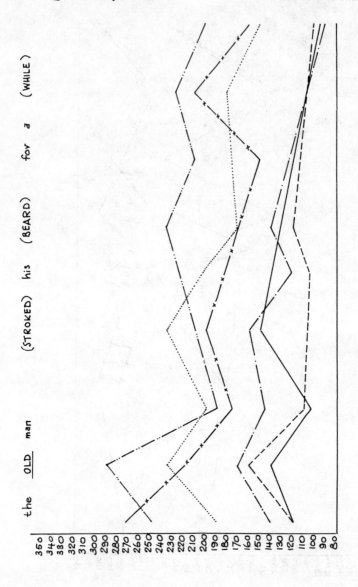

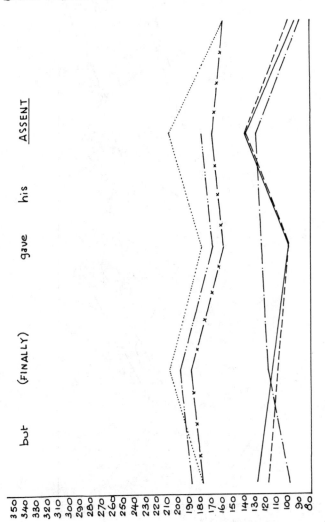

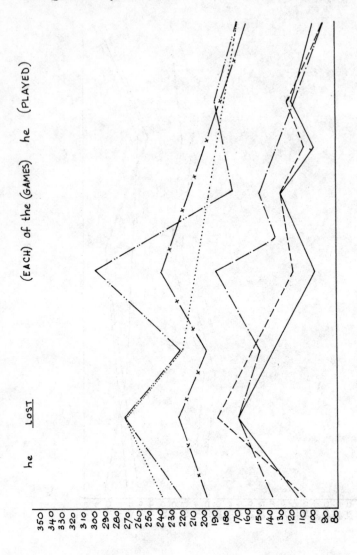

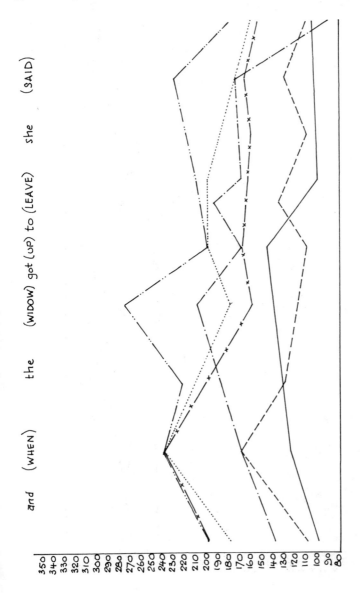

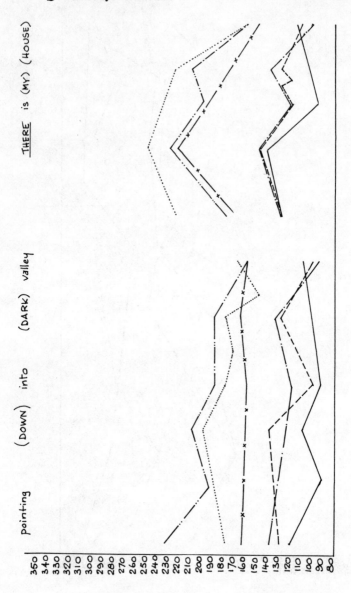

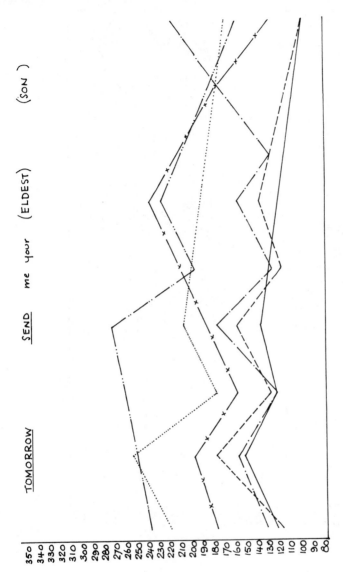

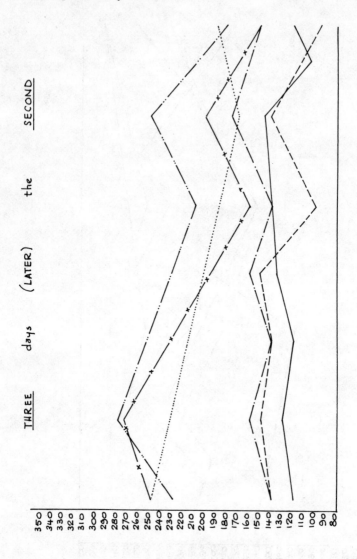

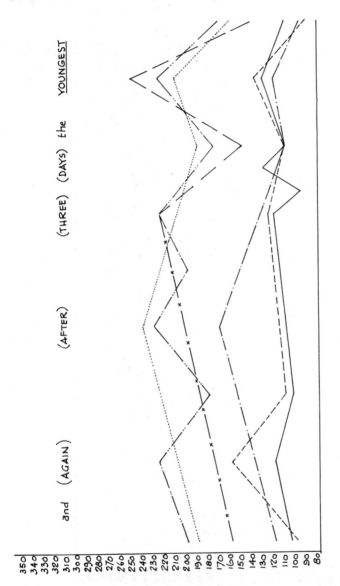

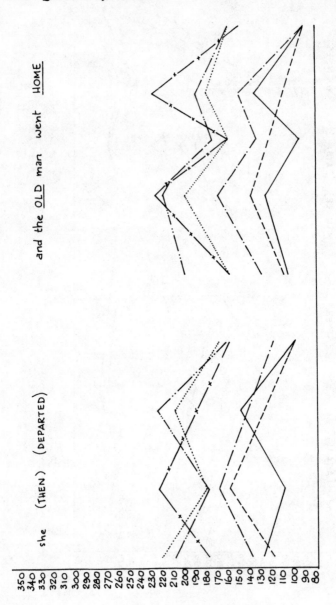

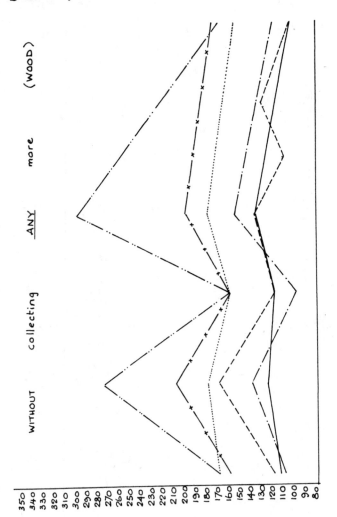

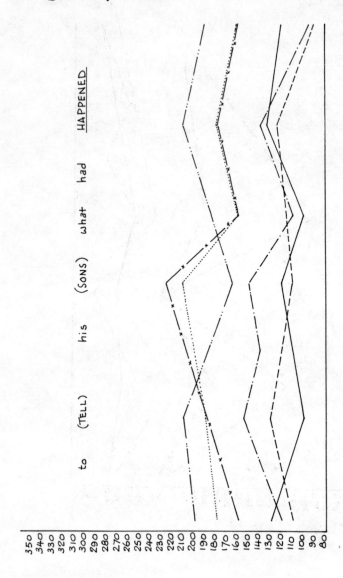

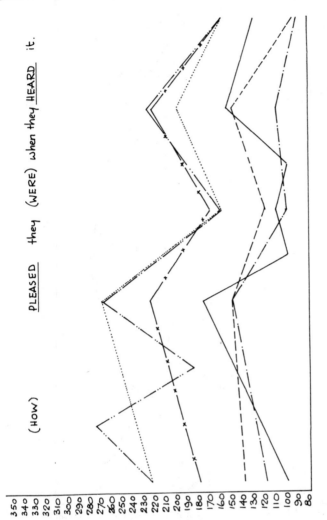

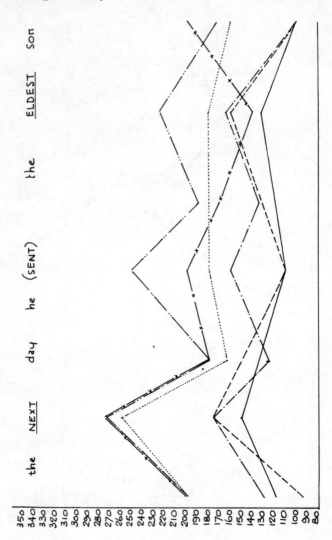

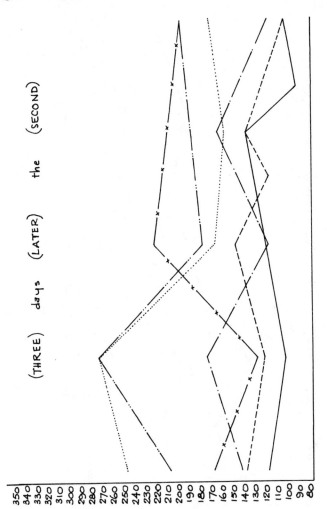

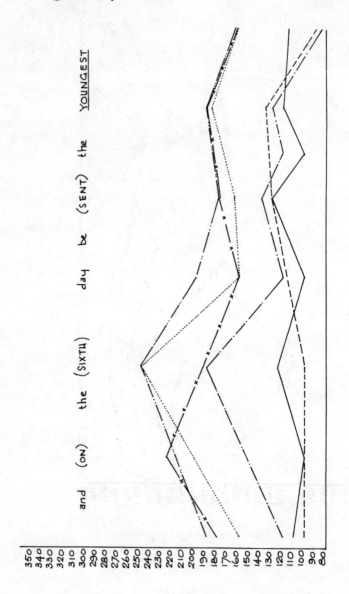

4.0. Intonation in Conversation

In 3.6. we examined some of the functions of intonation in structuring discourse. In particular we noted the way in which new topics and sub-topics were marked by a high peak on the first stressed word of a pause-defined unit with a consequent marked raising of the base-line. We noted too that the end of a sub-topic or topic was marked by a lowering of stressed peaks and a slight lowering of the base-line.

In this chapter we turn to look at the apparently systematic exploitation of this same set of intonational cues in conversational interaction between two participants.

4.1. Question-Answer Sequences

A very consistent pattern in the data occurs in the sequencing of questions and answers. The effect can be summarised thus: if the speaker asks a question high in his tessitura, boosting peaks and raising the base-line of the utterance, the hearer, when it is his turn to speak, replies high in his tessitura. On the other hand, if the speaker asks a question relatively low in his tessitura, the hearer, when he speaks, will respond relatively low.

We shall, for the moment, ignore the problem of deciding what is a question and simply discuss a series of utterances by A which are clearly responded to by B. We shall represent the intonation of these sequences in an impressionistic transcription, where the two bounding lines of the stave represent respectively the highest level and the lowest level the analyst believes the speaker will attain in normal speech. The level of unstressed syllables (of classes A and C (see 3.6.iv)) in each case realises the base-line of the utterance.

The first four utterances are raised high in the speaker's pitch range especially at the beginning of each contour.

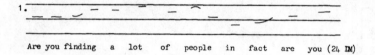

Are you finding   a   lot   of   people   in   fact   are   you (24 DM)

(KC has been telling DM how the interview is to be structured. DM interrupts her to ask this question.)

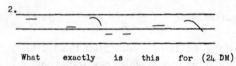

What   exactly   is   this   for (24 DM)

(DM has been reading a list of sentences. DM hands the sheet back to KC and asks this question.)

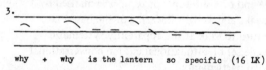

why + why   is the lantern   so   specific (16 LK)

(LK has been looking at the photograph of Edinburgh and trying to orient herself. This discussion has now ended, with LK saying I'd never have recognised that, never. There is then laughter, a pause, and LK asks this question.)

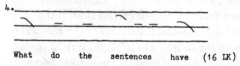

What   do   the   sentences   have   (16 LK)

(The interview has apparently been completed. KC has said thank you and LK laughs and comments very easy. Then LK asks this question.)
    The second set of utterances are placed much lower in the speaker's pitch range, noticeably so at the beginning of each contour. The first two speakers are those who produced the utterances in 1-4.

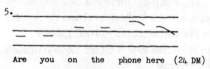

Are   you   on   the   phone here (24 DM)

(DM has promised to supply the names of potential subjects for the project. KC and DM are talking about how they will get in touch with each other.)

6.

Is that the + the art gallery   at the bottom   there (16 LK)

(LK is trying to orient herself during the discussion of the photograph of old Edinburgh.)

7.

am I   allowed   to read this   bit   at   the   back (11 MR)

(MR has noticed some writing on the back of the photograph during the discussion of the photograph.)

8.

they're having a fight are   they (11 MR)

(MR is looking at the photograph and commenting on what she observes.)

The pattern that we observe here seems quite consistent with that which we have already discussed in 3.6.ii. When the speaker changes the subject, the pitch of peaks and base-line rises. In three cases in examples 1-4 the speaker has reason to believe that an activity has been completed and he initiates a new topic (2 and 4) or re-starts an old one (3) or, in the case of 1, interrupts KC to initiate a topic which interests him. In the second set, 5-6, these questions arise out of the discussion and appear to be relevant continuations, obviously contributing to the same topic area.

When we examine the answers to these two sets of questions, we find that the pitch range of the speaker is regularly matched to that of the previous speaker. These are the replies to questions 1-4:

1.

em + some+ we haven't got   too many   from Morningside district   (KC)

2.

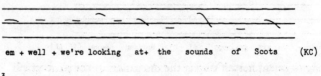

em + well + we're looking   at+   the   sounds   of   Scots   (KC)

3.

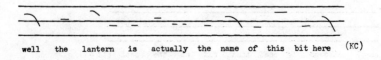

well   the   lantern   is   actually   the   name   of   this   bit   here   (KC)

4.

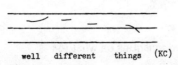

well   different   things   (KC)

In each case the onset is high. The onset regularly shows the speaker's unpreparedness for the question, since in each case the speaker begins by a 'channel holding filler' em or well which appears to signify that the speaker accepts the turn and will reply, but needs time to plan the reply.

In the next set of answers the onset to the answer is much lower:

5.

nope   (KC)

6.

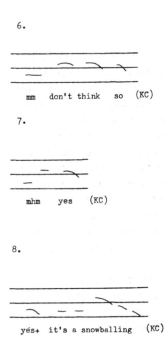

mm   don't think   so   (KC)

7.

mhm   yes   (KC)

8.

yés+ it's a snowballing   (KC)

These short answers, where the speaker merely answers yes or no with very little amplification and in each case has the obvious expectation that B will take back the turn and continue to speak on the same topic, all start low in the pitch range and stay fairly low.

All eight of these answers are spoken by KC, the interviewer. This same pattern, however, can be observed in conversations in which KC is not a participant, and in the game-playing sequences. It seems that participants in a conversation co-operate in signalling when they are about to embark on a new topic by raising pitch and a second speaker will then accept this new topic by, to begin with, also marking it by raising pitch — 'I realise you have broached a new topic and I am following your lead.' On the other hand, when both participants assume that what they are talking about is contained within an ongoing topic, they will both mark their assumption of this by remaining low in tessitura.

4.2. Extended Interaction

In this section we examine two extended stretches of interaction, first of all between one of our subjects, Mary Smith and KC. The speech produced by MS is analysed by the method described in 3.2.i. We have concentrated attention in this discussion on the range of Fo in initial position in the pause-defined unit. Figures for Fo readings are in general only given for words at the beginning and end of the unit. However some excursions from the base-line within a pause-defined unit are also noted. Figures below the words represent Fo in cps, figures above the words represent intensity readings measured in decibels. In general we shall make rather little comment on the intensity readings. In most cases high frequencies correlate with high-intensity readings and low with low. However there are some occasions, especially in turn-final position when this is not the case, and this we shall comment on.

Conventions — utterances under consideration are underlined. Fo readings are given below and intensity readings above the word. Utterances by the interviewer appear in brackets.

1.   (Could you give me your full name please)
　　　20　　20

2.   <u>Mary Smith</u> (fine — could you spell your last name)
　　　130　220

　　　31　24　22　20　24
3.   <u>S +M +I +T +H</u>　(uh huh and where were you born)
　　　150　　　　　110
　　　22 16 20

4.   <u>Edinburgh</u>　(and have you lived in Edinburgh all your life)
　　　120　220
　　　　　　20

5.   <u>All my life　uh huh</u> (fine — have you moved around within
　　　130　　100
　　　Edinburgh at all)
　　　22　20　　29　　　　　22　24
6.   <u>not really</u> + <u>always in the Gorgie area</u> (but have you moved from
　　　130　120　　160　　　　　110
　　　street to street at all)
　　　31
7.   <u>well yes uh huh I was born in I don't know if you know it</u>
　　　150
　　　Yeoman Place

8. and now I live in Westfield that's all (uh huh) hm (oh well —

                   12   27 22

                        120   100

    fine — where were your parents born)

9. em both Edinburgh (uh huh fine — so you're genuine Edinburgh)

      22 35 27   20

    130 215 140   100

10. well yes it's se+ third generation Irish perhaps so I don't know (laugh) because my grandparents came from Ireland on my mother's side (huh — fine — where did you go to school)

11. in Edinburgh (which sch. . .) in erm I went to St Cuthbert's

     20 20

    140   120

    primary school which is in Slateford and St Thomas' secondary school which is in Chalmers Street (uh huh fine do you have any children)

12. yes I have four (uh huh could you give me their names and ages)

    110   140

13. certainly Mark is seventeen Angel's fifteen Paul is thirteen and Kirstie is six (mm I like the name Kirstie + erm now then what schools do they go to) three are at St Augustine which is out at Broomhouse + well + between Broomhouse and Corstorphine one is at St Cuthbert's which is in Hutchison (fine and can you tell me how you get in from your home to here)

14. by bus unfortunately number two normally (laugh) sometimes

         30   24   30   30

    140   140 250 160   150   140

    a thirty five (and can you describe roughly the route that it takes to get in)

15. well either the Gorgie Road if I don't have to take my youngest

     35   35

    140   180

16. one to school but normally I take her to school in the morning

                  30   22   23   22

17. so I come in via Slateford into Fountainbridge (uh huh)

                 130   120

18. and up by the back of the Castle (oh) that way normally (fine)

                    16

                    100

[Photograph of old Edinburgh]

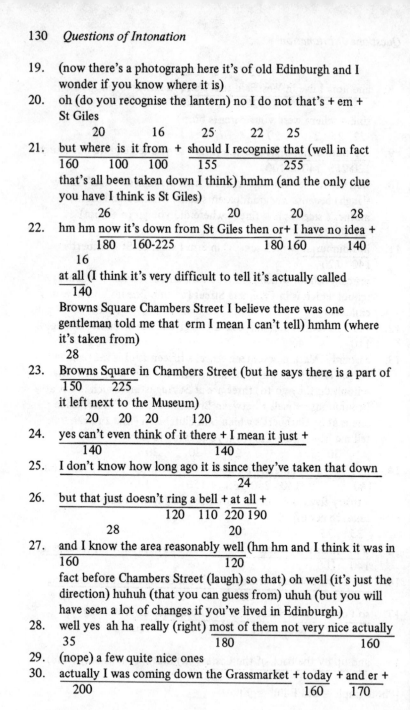

19. (now there's a photograph here it's of old Edinburgh and I
     wonder if you know where it is)

20. oh (do you recognise the lantern) no I do not that's + em +
     St Giles
              20   16   25   22   25

21. but where is it from + should I recognise that (well in fact
     160   100   100   155   255
     that's all been taken down I think) hmhm (and the only clue
     you have I think is St Giles)
              26   20   20   28

22. hm hm now it's down from St Giles then or+ I have no idea +
              180   160-225   180 160   140
        16
     at all (I think it's very difficult to tell it's actually called
     140
     Browns Square Chambers Street I believe there was one
     gentleman told me that erm I mean I can't tell) hmhm (where
     it's taken from)
       28

23. Browns Square in Chambers Street (but he says there is a part of
     150   225
     it left next to the Museum)
              20   20   20   120

24. yes can't even think of it there + I mean it just +
              140   140

25. I don't know how long ago it is since they've taken that down
                                          24

26. but that just doesn't ring a bell + at all +
                          120   110 220 190
        28   20

27. and I know the area reasonably well (hm hm and I think it was in
     160   120
     fact before Chambers Street (laugh) so that) oh well (it's just the
     direction) huhuh (that you can guess from) uhuh (but you will
     have seen a lot of changes if you've lived in Edinburgh)

28. well yes ah ha really (right) most of them not very nice actually
        35   180   160

29. (nope) a few quite nice ones

30. actually I was coming down the Grassmarket + today + and er +
     200   160   170

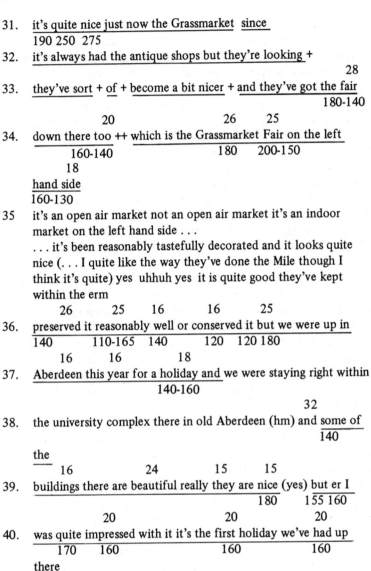

31. it's quite nice just now the Grassmarket since
190 250 275

32. it's always had the antique shops but they're looking +
28

33. they've sort + of + become a bit nicer + and they've got the fair
180-140

20   26   25

34. down there too ++ which is the Grassmarket Fair on the left
160-140   180   200-150
18

hand side
160-130

35   it's an open air market not an open air market it's an indoor
market on the left hand side . . .
. . . it's been reasonably tastefully decorated and it looks quite
nice (. . . I quite like the way they've done the Mile though I
think it's quite) yes uhhuh yes it is quite good they've kept
within the erm
26   25   16   16   25

36. preserved it reasonably well or conserved it but we were up in
140   110-165   140   120   120 180
16   16   18

37. Aberdeen this year for a holiday and we were staying right within
140-160

32

38. the university complex there in old Aberdeen (hm) and some of
140

the
16   24   15   15

39. buildings there are beautiful really they are nice (yes) but er I
180   155 160

20   20   20

40. was quite impressed with it it's the first holiday we've had up
170   160   160   160

there
160

The speaker's frequency range in this extract is from 100-275 cps,
i.e. she has a range of 175 cps. Whereas she frequently produces peaks
up to just over 200 cps, only once, in line 31, does she climb to 275 cps.

The interaction begins with a series of questions to which MS gives
short answers. Two of these short answers are uttered on a rise to high

in her voice range (line 2 and line 4). It is hard to see why she should choose to use rises rather than falls unless it is because she is aware that she is to be asked a series of questions and she uses the high rise as a signal that she expects more to come. It is a notable feature of her shorter utterances (e.g. lines 2, 4, 5, 6, 9 and 12) that they begin lower in her range than longer utterances. We should be careful of premature generalisation but it does seem that when the speaker has more ground to cover she begins higher. Whereas these short answers begin between 110 and 130 cps, longer ones begin between 140 and 160 cps.

Lines 15-18 nicely illustrate the speaker expecting that her hearer will share with her the increasing predictability of her bus route. Once she has elected to come into the town by Slateford the route is thoroughly determined. The falling peaks reflect this increasing predictability, <u>Slateford</u> (130) <u>Fountainbridge</u> (120) and <u>Castle</u> (100). Clearly she assumes that KC is familiar with the route of the number 2 bus.

It is clear that throughout most of the discussion of the photograph MS is not particularly interested in the topic. In 21 she produces <u>should I recognise that</u> with <u>that</u> rising to 255 cps, apparently in disbelief. And she reaffirms her negative feelings with <u>at all</u> in line 26 which falls from 220 to 190. KC, quickly responding to this rejection of the photograph as a topic, then produces (27) a garbled sort of apology for inflicting this photograph task on her and then proffers an ambivalent utterance <u>but you will have seen a lot of changes if you've lived in Edinburgh</u> which she utters quite low in her voice range, without marking this as the introduction of a new topic. MS appears to begin by taking this as a signing-off remark which she perfunctorily agrees to, also low in her pitch range. KC assumes that that is the end of the topic and utters a high and loud <u>right</u>, a clear boundary marker, but by this time MS has decided to keep the topic alive and makes a further comment. She begins high and loud (28) <u>most of them not very nice actually</u>, falls a bit on a few quite nice ones and then clearly marks her contribution to this topic with <u>actually</u>, peaking at 200 cps, staying high and loud throughout, <u>coming down the Grassmarket</u>, dropping a bit on <u>today + and + er</u> and going right up to 250 and 275 cps with her justification of this <u>quite nice</u> change in the Grassmarket. The effect of this peaking on <u>quite nice</u> (a phrase which is repeated from 29) is to make it very emphatic.

She peters out on this topic when it becomes obvious that KC is not familiar with the area she's talking about. KC takes a turn and suggests that the (Royal) Mile has been done up quite well too and MS politely agrees but without much enthusiasm or pitch movement, (35) preserved it reasonably well or conserved it (where conserved which might have been expected to contrast with preserved is treated as a synonym, 'given') and goes right on to add a new sub-topic beginning high on but (35) with Aberdeen as another example of an area with quite nice changes. Once past the introductory but there is not much pitch movement, just some slight variation between 160 and 180 cps and the speaker tails away high in her voice range, with low intensity. There is no clear end-of-turn marking.

It is clear from studying the recording of this interaction that it requires a great deal of co-operation and sensitivity for these two speakers to preserve a conversation. This was the first time they had met and for neither of them was the role entirely straightforward. MS was doing KC a 'favour' by coming and talking to her, and yet KC was on her own ground and in charge of the interview. Their perceptions of how the conversation is progressing are clearly not exactly matched. KC is obviously embarrassed at the failure of the photograph and MS's evident distaste for this task, and is quite ready to give up the interview in line 27 but feels obliged to utter the remark about changes in Edinburgh which has provoked so much successful conversations in so many interviews. MS seems to feel that she has had enough, but then starts opening up the conversation again in 30. She battles on through a rather tricky bit in 34 right up to 39, and then leaves it up to KC to decide whether to continue or not. KC does in fact come back with a tentative comment on yet another set of cleaned-up buildings in Edinburgh, but this time MS picks up her turn with a comment very low in her range, and at this KC begins to thank her for coming. It can certainly be claimed that this interchange does not exemplify interaction at its most comfortable and successful. On the other hand it must be admitted that this sort of somewhat awkward conversation where roles are not clearly defined and people are 'talking for the sake of talking' is a not uncommon experience of everyday life.

The next extract comes from a much more comfortable interaction where the speaker (LK) is talking animatedly about her experiences over the Christmas holidays. KC says of her holiday in the Borders, We didn't have much snow this winter — did you have snow in Edinburgh? LK then proceeds:

1.   I was away + all Christmas holidays
2.   (whereabouts)

3.
  26   28   32   28   24
  down in Derbyshire (oh) where they had gales and the rain and
  140   160   140   160   150

4.
      30   32   26   30
  the floods and the + pub we went to actually on erm Old Year's
  150 140-150
      22
  Night

5.
                      28   24
  was + no ele- + there was no electricity and there was
  140   180-140   135 150   140

6.
  28   24
  trees and everything over the road + it was quite frightening
                      165   160   180

7. (terrible)

8.
        30 32 32   30   28
  yeah but we didn't see snow till we came up + the motorway +
      180   160-140   150-120

9.
        28   20   16   16
  the snow ploughs were out over Shap (were they) yeah +
      210   140   155

10.
  25   29   20   20   20
  the first time I've ever seen snow ploughs on a motorway +
      200   145

11.
            27 27   21
  it was quite + quite amazing (crikey)
      160   150-165

12.
  18   27 32   18   18   18
  but I don't know if we'll get any this year or not + I hope not
  215   140-160

13. (you had quite a good holiday) oh super (apart from the storm)

14. really super the English fairly showed us how to bring in

15. the New Year (oh yes, did they) yes they do it in a much
                                      245

16. more I think civilised way +

17. they have you round to dances + local dances + each
                              22   32   35   30   32

18. little village has a dance (hmmm) and they don't go visiting
                              135 140 190 150 180-140

	16 16				22	26	32
19.	so much except on + the next day they go round to people's

140   160   130   150   180-140

   24   22 29 24   30 30   22 30

20.   houses (hm hm) but eh it was very good (ah ha) and very

    140   180 130 140 180 150   160 160

   26

21.   friendly + and nobody got too obstreperous as they do here

   140-130

   (laugh)

   28   26   18   18

22.   but I — I thoroughly enjoyed myself (good great)

   160   120-140   140   140

Once again the utterances under consideration are underlined, frequency readings appear below words and intensity readings above.

The pitch range of this speaker lies between 120 cps and 300 cps but in this extract it rarely drops as low as 120 cps and only once, in line 15, goes above 215 cps. The speaker's utterance is characterised by the frequent use of perceptually quite level pitch — even instrumentally there is little variation. These level pitches occur most obviously at the end of pause-defined sequences which precede further utterance on the same topic (e.g. lines 3, 4, 19 and 20).

This speaker uses what seems to be a common strategy in our data to warn her interlocutor that she has not finished speaking when the syntax appears to be completed and a complete rational utterance has been achieved. So at the end of line 6, it was quite frightening, the pitch rises on frightening and again, in line 11, it was quite + quite amazing, the pitch rises on amazing and in line 12, in this year or not, it rises on or not. It is not until I hope not (line 12) that the speaker produces a fall in pitch and a rapid diminution in intensity. We are familiar with the instruction to children reading aloud to 'keep the voice up at commas' where the assumption is that more to come must be signalled intonationally as well as syntactically. In speech it is very common to find that the intonation falls (though perhaps not right to the base-line) when the syntax clearly marks incompletion, but rises when the syntax marks completion in the case where the speaker wishes to maintain his turn.

In the second half of this extract LK responds enthusiastically to KC's polite and high you had quite a good holiday with a high peak on super and then several emphatic utterances culminating in line 18, and

they don't go visiting so much, where don't, peaking at 190 cps, is heard
as clearly contrastive — remember a Scottish girl is talking to another
about how the English celebrate New Year. (Those unfamiliar with
Scottish culture should know that New Year's Eve, 'Hogmanay', is
traditionally the occasion of considerable celebration in Scotland.)
At the end of this section we have another example of the
phenomenon we observed in the previous speaker who produced a
signing off phrase it's the first holiday we've had up there with marked
diminution of intensity, reduction of pitch movement but no fall to low
in pitch height. LK's last utterance, I thoroughly enjoyed myself,
similarly presents very narrow pitch variation, considerable diminution
of intensity but very level pitch at 140 cps. (This speaker can fall
lower — she has after all produced levels at 130 cps in lines 19, 20 and
21.) In particular, there is clearly no fall to low at the end of the
speaker's turn. We remarked on the same phenomenon in the speech of
22 BS in 3.6.ii. We might attribute this to the uncertainty of structure
which the unfamiliar interview situation imposes on the speaker.
However, we believe it to be more generally characteristic of a hesitant
giving-up of turn when the speaker feels that perhaps the conversation
should continue but there is no clear sign that his interlocutor is about
to take a turn.

We have presented some evidence in this brief chapter of some of the
ways in which speakers use intonation as signals to their interlocutors.
It seems to us quite clear that the overriding use of intonation is to allow
the speaker to give notice of how he views the topic under discussion.
He must mark a new topic or sub-topic by raising initial stressed peaks.
If the preceding speaker announces a new topic, for example in a
question, the speaker will echo that 'new topic' marker to show that he
assigns this the same status. If the preceding speaker treats a topic as
ongoing, the new speaker will continue the ongoing status low in his
pitch range unless he has to contradict something the previous speaker
has assumed, in which case he will speak contrastively. We find then,
evidence of co-operation between speakers in a conversation to signal
change, or maintain the status, of topic.

We should note that our analysis bears a close resemblance to that of
Brazil (1978) who has examined the role of 'key' in discourse. The
notion of key derives from Sweet (1906) who claims that 'each
sentence or sentence group has a general pitch or key of its own . . .
Change of key has a purely logical significance. Thus questions are
naturally uttered in a higher key than answers, and parenthetic clauses
in a lower key than those which state the main facts. In all natural

speech there is incessant change of key.' Brazil follows Sweet in recognising three levels of key — high, mid and low. He makes several insightful comments, for instance: 'Any occurrence of a high-key tone group can be thought of as phonetically bound to a succeeding tone group; any low-key tone group as bound to the preceding one.' We agree with much that Brazil says, but find no compelling reason for wanting to recognise three levels of key. On the contrary, we find evidence, of the sort we have discussed in this chapter, for two levels: one level which marks the introduction of a new topic by a shift-up in key, and a second which marks an ongoing topic by remaining low in key. It is not clear what the third member of a set which includes topic-initial and ongoing-topic might be (as indeed Brazil's remarks, quoted above, imply).

5

5.0. The Tonic

The notion of 'nuclear' or 'tonic' syllable or word is well established in British descriptions of intonation. It is adumbrated in Coleman (1914) who writes of 'the chief word' of a sentence, and the notion of a nucleus is explored in detail by Palmer (1922). Later scholars, notably Halliday (1967, 1968, 1970) and Crystal (1969, 1975) have leaned on this notion in their descriptions of English intonation. We should note two points: the first is that the early descriptions were based, apparently, on sentences cited in isolation. The second is that all these authors are discussing RP. We have already pointed out (2.7.) that RP is distinguished by having an inclined base-line and considerable movement on the last stressed syllables which tends to make the last stressed item prominent in a way which is not true of, say, ESE. A further point to note is that descriptions of American English intonation do not, typically, make appeal to this notion. Pike (1945), using as data readings of 'conversational prose', identifies 'four relative but significant levels [pitch phonemes] . . . which serve as the basic building blocks for intonation contours'. He then identifies *primary types* of contour which typically occur on the last lexical item in a sentence which he reasonably enough identifies as 'finality contours'. Trager and Smith (1951) and Chomsky and Halle (1968) also deal in configurations of pitch level rather than a particular contour type which is 'placed' within a unit.*

The characteristic contours which are said to contrast on the tonic (or nuclear) syllable (or word) in British descriptions are, in most descriptions, assigned a 'meaning' of some kind even if it is only to distinguish between 'finality' and 'more to come' (Hultzen, 1959) or 'speaker assumes is known to the listener' versus 'speaker assumes is not known to the listener' (Brazil, 1978). Quite apart from these meanings, which are carried by individual tones or tunes, the placing of the tonic within a tone group is said to be significant in itself (see 2.4.) since this,

*Chomsky and Halle do of course claim to be assigning 'stress levels' rather than 'pitch levels' but it is by no means clear how this distinction is to be drawn.

it is claimed, reflects the information structure of the unit. The tonic will mark what is 'new' in the utterance whereas that which is not marked as new is treated as 'given'. It is clearly crucial, in such a theory (and the theories of Halliday, 1967 and Chafe, 1970 both embrace this view) that the hearer is able to distinguish which part of the tone group is the tonic, thus what the speaker is treating as new and what he assumes that the listener already shares or can be expected, in Halliday's terms, to 'recover'. The importance of this view of information structure has been stressed in a long series of experiments by Clark (discussed in Clark and Clark, 1977) who leans on Halliday's account of the tonic. Clark claims that the hearer must use what is marked as given to find the relevant address in memory and add to this address the information which the speaker marks as new. Indeed he claims that there exists a 'given-new contract' which exists between speaker and hearer which is precisely specified: 'i) the speaker agrees to use given information to refer to information (s)he thinks the listener can uniquely identify from what he already knows and ii) to use new information to refer to information (s)he believes to be true but is not already known to the speaker.'*

It is clearly important, in this view, for the hearer to be able to identify the tonic item within a tone group, otherwise he is denied crucial cues to information structure. How does it come about then that we have such difficulty in identifying items as tonics in the spontaneous speech that we describe in Chapter 3? And how does it come about that, having this difficulty, we still have no problems in understanding what the speaker is saying and hence, presumably, sorting out the information structure satisfactorily? In the next sections of this chapter we describe a series of pilot experiments which were carried out to see whether native speakers who knew what tonics were, and were confident of their ability to recognise one when they heard one, would in fact agree with each other in their identification of the tonic.

We were interested not only in whether our subjects would agree

---

*Clark's view of what is given has been correctly criticised by Chafe (1976). Chafe points out that in many of Clark's experiments, which typically involve pairs of constructed sentences presented to subjects, it is often the case that what Clark describes as given is simply 'definite'. Thus in the much-discussed experiment which includes the pair of sentences

Mary got some picnic supplies out of the car
The beer was warm

(discussed in Clark and Clark, 1977), Chafe suggests that there is no question of the beer being given. 'Givenness' is not the category which is at issue here.

about where the tonic(s) was placed in a given chunk of speech but also in what cues they were using to identify the tonic. There is considerable agreement in the literature about which phonetic features identify the tonic. Halliday (1970) identifies the tonic thus:

> The tonic syllable is often longer, and may be louder, than the other salient syllables in the tone group: what makes it prominent, however, is neither length nor loudness but the fact that it plays the principal part in the intonation of the tone group. The tonic syllable carries the main burden of pitch movement in the tone group, and it does this in one of two ways. Usually this means that it covers the *widest pitch range* . . . The alternative possibility is for it to occur *immediately following a pitch jump*, where instead of a continuous rising or falling movement there is a jump up or down (a musical interval) between syllables.

Other scholars, working within different theoretical frameworks also mention maximum pitch movement but, in general, insist also on maximum pitch height and maximum intensity (see Fry, 1958; Hadding-Koch and Studdert-Kennedy, 1965; Denes and Milton-Williams, 1962; Morton and Jassem, 1965). Some scholars have also included duration as a parameter (see Burgess, 1973; Denes and Milton-Williams, 1962; Peterson and Lehiste, 1960). But there is a problem with measuring duration if one is dealing with utterances longer than monosyllables or utterances which are not produced by a speech synthesiser. Clearly what we are interested in is relative duration, but with speech from texts read aloud or, even more difficult, spontaneous speech, it is not clear how it is possible to establish a norm of duration for a given syllable type, within a given lexical class, under specified conditions of degree of stress and placing in intonation contour, within a given sentence structure, spoken by the same speaker in the same manner. We have therefore not included duration as a parameter for examination in the work described in this chapter. The phonetic cues which we have examined are A (maximum pitch height), B (maximum pitch movement) and C (maximum intensity).

Each chunk of speech which was examined in the experiments described here was submitted to instrumental analysis of the sort described in Chapter 3. Within each chunk (usually a short sentence) the syllable with maximum Fo was identified and labelled A, that with maximum movement was labelled B and that with maximum intensity was labelled C. Where two equal maximum peaks of Fo or intensity were recorded within the same chunk, both peaks were assigned the label A or C and where two equal maximum amounts of Fo movement were recorded each syllable was labelled B. So, for example, sentence 14 in Figure 5.1, How many children have you though, yields three maxima of Fo movement (measured in cps), how children and have. How peaks highest in Fo and children has maximum intensity. We describe this sentence, for the purposes of our experiments, thus:

How (AB) many children (BC) have (B) you though

Each sentence in the data was labelled in this way. There are often problems in assigning the readings to specific syllables rather than to longer stretches but we were reasonably confident that the readings were assigned correctly within a particular word. The subjects were, then, always asked to identify tonic words rather than syllables. The chunks they were asked to make judgements about were complete sentences. No tone group division was suggested or assigned to these sentences — in all cases subjects were allowed to assign more than one tonic within a sentence if they wished to do so, with no limit on the number of tonics.

The experiments we describe in the next sections must be regarded as pilot experiments. The number of judges varies from one experiment to the next,* and we do not have a sufficient number to justify the statistical operations which would be necessary to show that our results were reliable and what their level of significance is. None the less, it seems worthwhile to report the experiments that we undertook, and their results, since they do seem to provide some ancillary evidence for the claims we made about the identification of the tonic in Chapter 3 and for the reformulation of tonic function that we offer in 5.4.

5.1. Experiment 1 — Tonics in ESE Sentences Read Aloud

Six ESE speakers with no linguistic training were asked to read a set of fifteen sentences. The sentences were presented out of context numbered 1-15 as they are presented in Appendix A. The sentences were analysed instrumentally and labelled in the manner we have

*We are particularly grateful to patient and co-operative colleagues among the staff and postgraduate students of the Department of Linguistics, Edinburgh, for their helpfulness and willingness to act as judges for us, in many cases on several different occasions.

already described. Out of these 90 sentences 22 yielded a combination of all the phonetic maxima (A, B and C) on the same syllable, 25 yielded AC on one syllable and B on another, 15 yielded A, B and C on different syllables, 14 yielded AB/C and 8 yielded A/BC. The remaining six yielded more complex patterns. It seems to be the case that, for ESE speakers, maximum Fo is more often associated with maximum intensity than with maximum movement.

From these sentences 20 were selected to exemplify the range of distribution of the phonetic maxima:

ABC	— 7 times (cumulation of all PM (phonetic maxima))
A/B/C	— 4 times (competition between each maximum)
B/AC	— twice
AC/ABC	— once
AB/C	— twice
AB/BC/B	— once
AB/AC	— once
AC/BC	— once
A/BC	— once

This range would enable us to see whether the judges would always prefer ABC as tonic where it was present and, when the cues were competing, which cues they preferred.

Twenty-nine judges made decisions about tonic-placing in this experiment. Eight were professional phoneticians, four were postgraduate students working on phonetic areas and the remainder were postgraduate students of the department who were professional teachers of English. All of this latter group claimed to be familiar with and to use in their teaching some description of English intonation which depended on the notion of tonic or nucleus. All of those taking part were confident, before they confronted the data, that they could easily identify tonics.

In each case the judges were asked to list the criteria that they thought they relied on before they listened to the data. They listed such features as 'maximum moving pitch, maximum pitch height, maximum change of pitch' as well as associated features of 'maximum length, maximum loudness' and the non-phonetic cue of 'last lexical item'. We noticed that judges from different accent-areas of the English-speaking world did not always choose the same parameter as criterial as judges from other areas. (We discuss this briefly at the end of this section.)

The judges were presented with a sentence which they heard three times with 8-second intervals between each presentation. They were told to underline the tonic word on the accompanying text. If they perceived more than one word as tonic they were to underline as many tonics as they wished. They heard two sample sentences and were asked if they had any problems before they began with the first sentence.

The results are presented in Figure 5.1. In each case, where judges identified one and only one tonic, the number of judges who choose a particular word is written below the word. Where judges identified more than one tonic the number appears in a second row enclosed in brackets. Thus, the first sentence, Have you change of a pound,* twenty-two of the twenty-nine judges choose only one tonic, nineteen choose pound and three choose change. The remaining seven judges choose two tonics. The bracketed number (7) under change indicates that it was chosen as one of two tonics. In sentence 10, May I watch the game, twenty judges choose game as the sole tonic, four choose may, three watch and one I and the twenty-ninth chooses all three words, may, watch and game as tonics.

Figure 5.1

1. Have you change(C) of a pound(AB)
                3   19
            (7)   (7)

2. Three(AC) sons (ABC)
    2   24
  (3)   (3)

3. Have you change(AC) of a pound(B)
              5   20
          (4)   (4)

4. There(ABC) is my house
  12   14
  (3)   (3)

5. How pleased(AC) they were they heard(AB) it
    9   10
  (9)   (1)   (10)

6. There(AB) is my(C) house
  2   27

*This is the standard Scottish equivalent to the standard English Have you (got) change for a pound.

7. The old(A) man(C) asked if she had posted(B) the letter
                            2   7   15
          (3)   (2)   (5)   (4)

8. He played(AC) squash(B) on Mondays, Wednesdays and Fridays
        1   4   16
       (1)   (8)   (7)

9. Three(ABC) sons
       27   2

10. May(C) I(A) watch the game(B)
       4   1   3   20
      (1)   (1)   (1)

11. How many(ABC) children do you have
          1   27   1

12. He lost(A) each(B) of the games(C) they played
       11   3   3   3
       (4)   (2)   (9)   (4)

13. He played(ABC) squash on Mondays, Wednesdays and Fridays
        9   7   9
       (1)   (4)   (4)

14. How(AB) many children(BC) have(B) you though
       4   2   16   2
      (2)   (1)   (4)   (1)   (1)   (1)

15. May I(A) watch the game(BC)
        10   4   12
       (3)   (3)

16. Do you want to play(ABC) with me
                    27
       (1)   (2)   (1)

17. How(A) many(C) children(B) do you have
                   27   1   1

18. I have three(AC) daughters(BC)
           7   18
      (1)   (3)   (4)

19. How pleased(ABC) they were when they heard it
          27   1
         (1)   (1)

20. He lost(ABC) each of the games they played
        4   1   17
       (6)   (2)   (6)   (2)

We shall briefly comment on the results of this experiment. In four out of the seven cases of cumulated ABC there is a clear majority of preference for cumulated ABC (2, 9, 16 and 19). However, in 4, 13 and 20 the majority is much less clear. In 4, a strong tendency to choose the last lexical item in the absence of any extremely strong phonetic cues on other items which characterised some judges' preferences is made clear. In 13 and 20 the picture is muddied by the possibility of internal division into several tone groups. There is obviously considerable disagreement in these cases.

In the next group, where A, B and C are dispersed over three items (sentences 7, 10, 12 and 17), there is a tendency to prefer the last lexical item whether or not it has any phonetic maximum on it (e.g. in 7 — in 10 and 17 the last lexical item in each case has B, maximum pitch movement). In 12 it seems clear that each competing stressed item serves as a potential tonic for someone.

Where AB competes with C in 1, AB, which cumulate on the last lexical item, wins hands down. In 6, however, where they cumulate on the initial deictic there, they only attract two votes and all the rest go to the last lexical item.

Where AC compete with B, B wins where it occurs on the last lexical item (3), and still wins over AC in 8, but loses to the phrases containing the last lexical item (six judges underlined the whole time constituent on Mondays, Wednesdays and Fridays).

In general when B occurs on the last lexical item this is chosen as tonic by twenty or more of the twenty-nine judges (1, 2, 3, 4, 10, 14, 16, 17 and 18). The last lexical item without B attracts twenty or more votes (6, 8 and 11). B alone, on an item other than the last lexical item, does consistently attract some votes (sentence 7 (12), 8 (12), 12 (5), 14 (3)) but not a majority. A (maximum height), especially in conjunction with C (intensity) also fairly consistently attracts votes (sentence 2 (5), 5 (18), 7 (3), 8 (2), 10 (1), 12 (15), 15 (13), 18 (10)) but only on two occasions wins a majority.

In thirteen out of the twenty sentences at least 75 per cent of judges agreed in the identification of at least one tonic. In the remaining seven sentences at least 50 per cent of judges agreed on at least one tonic (sentences 4, 5, 7, 12, 13, 14 and 15) but in this second set there was a considerable spread of choice.

Conclusions

1. Judges will choose the last lexical item as tonic if there is no strong phonetic competition elsewhere in the sentence (nine sentences). They

will sometimes choose the last lexical item if all the phonetic maxima are located elsewhere in the sentence. It appears, then, that the last lexical item is regarded as being the tonic *by right of being the last lexical item* if some other item is not heavily marked phonetically as being in competition.

2. In no case, even in two-word sentences, was only one tonic identified. In all cases the judges, between them, identified at least two tonics and usually three, four or five. Any item perceived as stressed seems to be at risk. Judges reported that they found the task a very difficult one — this was true even of seasoned phoneticians who have been teaching intonation for years. Note that this implies a problem with recognising the number of tone groups within the sentence.

3. It was noticeable that Americans and Scots (eight of them) tended to choose the item with maximum pitch height whereas RP speakers (nine of them) tended to prefer maximum pitch movement. Since these maxima quite rarely coincide this means that speakers of the same language are using cues which will guide them to different items. Can it be the case that they do this in normal speech and have different strategies for processing the same incoming information structure?

4. It is clear that the expectation, often voiced in the literature and properly attacked by Schmerling (1974), that there is a 'normal' stress and intonation which will be applied to sentences read out of context, is misplaced. Whereas in the text read aloud, which we discussed in the previous section, there was a large measure of agreement between readers, in sentences read out of context there is no constraining context and the reader-aloud, like the judge, is free to invent his own. This leads to considerable variation both as measured instrumentally and as judged by our judges. Consider the two sentences 5 and 19:

5. How pleased(AC) they were, when they heard(AB) it
          9   10
         (9)   (1)   (10)
19. How pleased(ABC) they were when they heard it
          27   1
         (1)   (1)

Similarly we find a difference between sentences 12 and 20:

12. He lost(A) each(B) of the games(C) they played

	11	3		3		3
	(4)	(2)		(9)		(4)

20. He lost(ABC) each of the games they played

	4		1		17	
	(6)		(2)		(6)	(2)

It seems quite clear that each of these sentences bears many interpretations if it is cited in isolation and that none of them can be claimed as 'the norm'.

5. We have given the Fo measurements in cps measured on a linear scale. It might be objected that a logarithmic scale would be more appropriate to model a perceptual scale. We can find in the literature little hard evidence on this and work done on the mel scale (Stevens *et al.* 1937, 1940) indeed suggests that at the relatively low frequencies which we are concerned with a linear scale is more appropriate. However even if it can be shown that the scale we have used is not ideal, we believe that under any scale the same maximum peaks will be identified. The problem will arise with determining whether a smaller Fo movement lower in the frequency scale is perceptually more salient than a larger movement higher in the frequency scale.

5.2. Experiment 2 – Tonics in Spontaneous Speech

The data for this second experiment was drawn from recordings of a game-playing situation in which one participant was given the text of a story and the other was given jumbled lists of characters and actions in the story and asked to reconstruct the story asking only yes/no questions. (The story and instructions to players are presented at the end of this chapter.) The game had been invented in the first place to enlarge the number of interrogatives and clefts in our data. (Both of these sentence types occur very rarely in our conversational data.) This data seemed particularly appropriate to our investigation of the location of tonics since the effect of a clefting transformation is held to be to focus syntactically a particular constituent of the sentence by bringing it to the front of the sentence. The general expectation then is that the constituent thus syntactically focused will be phonologically marked as the tonic. Thus, for instance, 'A special construction which gives both thematic and focal prominence to a particular element of the clause is the cleft sentence . . . The usefulness of the cleft sentence resides partly in its unambiguous marking of the focus of information in written English, where the clue of intonation is absent. The highlighted element has the full implication of contrastive focus: the rest of the clause is taken as given, and a contrast is inferred with other items which might have filled the focal or "hinge" position in the sentence.' (Quirk, Greenbaum, Leech and Svartvik, 1972). The other advantage of this data was that it provided a large number of examples of formally contrastive utterances, since a player would start out with the hypothesis that it was say, the old man who had three sons and, on being told that it was not, he would then ask whether it was the rich farmer (contrast) who had three sons. We recorded six of these games, and used utterances produced by three speakers, two male ESE speakers and one female RP speaker for this experiment.

Our expectation was that items in formal contrast would be realised with a cumulation of phonetic maxima and would be identified by the judges in preference to the last lexical item. Our expecation was, further, that items which were syntactically focused would tend to be phonologically focused but, since the syntactic cue was manifest, the phonological cues might not be so marked as they have to be in marking contrast.

Once again we selected twenty utterances from the data and we chose fluent, syntactically coherent chunks which, in general, constitute sentences. Of these, eleven were cleft sentences (in general cleft questions), seven were non-cleft but contrastive and the remaining two were non-cleft and non-contrastive.

In this experiment twenty-five judges selected tonics, a sub-set of the group in Experiment 1. Their instructions, as in Experiment 1, were to underline any item which they identified as a tonic. Once again they heard each item three times with an 8-second interval between them.

Figure 5.2

1. The pony(ABC) runs away
            25
2. Was it the miller's daughter(ABC) who returns home on the back
            9
        (7)   (3)

     of the pony
         9
       (7)

3. Presumably it was the eldest(ABC) son
                      25

4. The second(ABC) son married the miller's daughter(AB)
        2   12
      (11)   (11)

5. Was it the youngest son(ABC) who tells his wife to carry the
                    8
             (11)

     saddle
      6
     (11)

6. Did the rich farmer(ABC) have three sons
           23
        (2)   (2)

7. Was it the second son(AC) who married the miller's daughter(B)
           12   6
        (7)   (7)

8. The dog(ABC) runs away
     23   2

9. Was it one of the sons(ABC) who was very well off
          23
        (2)   (2)

10. Was it the rich farmer's eldest son(ABC) who married the
                23
         (2)

     gentleman's daughter

        (2)

11. It was the eldest(ABC) son
          25

12. Was it the youngest(ABC) son that married(A) the very beautiful
         20
       (5)   (1)
     miller's daughter

       (4)

13.   Was it the miller's(ABC) daughter who was very beautiful then
             23
             (2)   (2)

14.   Was it the wife of the newly married couple who was
                                          5
                                         (13)
      impressed(AB) by previous events and became a very obedient

                              (4)   (1)
      wife(AC)
        6
      (12)

15.   Was it the bad-natured daughter(ABC) who ran away
                          21   2
                         (2)   (2)

16.   Is it the miller's(ABC) dog
             25

17.   Well did the old man(ABC) have three sons(AB)
                    5   7
             (2)   (12)   (12)

18.   Is it the pony(ABC) who refuses to cross a stream and is shot(AB)
             11   5
             (8)   (3)   (8)

19.   Was it the rich farmer(BC) who had three sons(A)
             10   8
             (7)   (7)

20.   So they got(ABC) married
         1   24

It is immediately obvious that the speakers in these sentences are
concentrating the phonetic cues in a way which was not true of the
typical sentence in Experiment 1. In 17 out of these 20 sentences all
the phonetic maxima cumulate on one item (the exceptions are 7, 14
and 19). It is also immediately obvious that the judges, despite the
greater length of many of these sentences, are identifying fewer tonics.

Let us first of all examine the contrastive non-cleft sentences (1, 3,
6, 8, 11, 16 and 20). In all cases the phonetic maxima cumulate on the
contrastive item. In 1, 3, 11 and 16 the judges unanimously choose the
contrasted item. In 6, all the judges choose <u>farmer</u> but two also choose
the last lexical item, <u>sons</u>. In 8, twenty-three judges and in 20, twenty-
four judges select the contrasted item. It is obviously the case that the
speakers have unambiguously marked the contrast in these sentences

and nearly all of the judges have consistently recognised this.

If we turn to the clefts we find a more complicated picture. Five of the clefts have phonetic maxima cumulating on one item and a clear majority of judges choosing this item (4, 9, 10, 12, 13 and 15). In all these cases it seems quite clear that the clefted constituent is in contrast with a previous guess by the speaker. In these clearly contrastive clefts the contrasted item is clearly marked phonetically by the speaker and identified by the judges.

Three further clefts (2, 5 and 18) also contain a cumulation of phonetic maxima on the clefted constituent but this time the judges split their votes between this item and another item (but note that this clefted item never receives less than sixteen votes). In all these sentences the clefted constituent has been mentioned previously by the speaker. In 2, miller's daughter was mentioned in the previous sentence and the remaining constituents are mentioned for the first time. In 5, youngest son is mentioned two sentences earlier and the other constituents are mentioned for the first time. In 18, pony has been mentioned earlier and the other constituents are mentioned for the first time. It seems, then, that here we have topic-structure, (given/ new) interacting with contrastiveness to diminish the effect of contrastiveness. It is true that 2, 5 and 18 are long sentences each containing at least three major constituents but this is also true of other long sentences where one item was none the less identified by a clear majority of judges as the tonic (e.g. 10 and 12). In 2, 5 and 18, both the given contrasted item and the new non-contrastive last lexical item are identified as tonics.

The three remaining cleft sentences (7, 14 and 19) split the phonetic maxima. In 7, both second son and miller's daughter are new and, although there is preference for second son, seven of the judges identify two tonics here. 14 is, of course, a very long sentence and it is hardly surprising that judges choose several tonics. This sentence was included to see whether the fact of a constituent being syntactically focused would still force judges to prefer it even in a very long structure and in competition with a new last constituent. In the event the judges split their votes evenly between the two. In 19, rich farmer has maximum height and is mentioned for the first time. Once again the votes split evenly.

The last two non-cleft, non-contrastive sentences (4 and 17) show the familiar effect we recognised in Experiment 1 of competing maxima and competing choices — clearly the judges are recognising two loci of prominence here.

Conclusions

1. Where contrast is involved only phonetic cues are available to mark it. The phonetic cues therefore cumulate on this item and the judges regularly recognise only one tonic, the contrasted element, even in a long structure (e.g. 10 and 12).

2. Where a clefted constituent is not marked by the speaker as being contrastive and a later constituent in the sentence is marked as new, the majority of judges will identify two tonic loci — one on the clefted element and one on the new constituent (e.g. 2, 5 and 7). It seems then the position held by Quirk *et al.*, quoted above, is too strong. It is indeed the case that the clefted constituent may be contrasted and the remaining constituents in the clause treated as given. But it is also the case that the clefted item may be uttered by the speaker in a context where the remaining constituents of the clause are new. In this case two loci of focus will be perceived in the utterance.

5.3. Further Experiments

A series of three further pilot experiments was constructed, in these cases using only the speech of RP speakers. Since the descriptions of the intonation of British English which we have discussed all describe the intonation of RP it seemed that we ought to attack directly the question of whether judges would more readily identify tonics in RP than in ESE. A series of twenty sentences was extracted from the games which we have already described. In the first of these three experiments judges were presented with forty sentences cited out of context and asked to underline the tonics on the accompanying text just as in the experiments already described. It was clear from the spread of judgements in this task that judges found it as hard to identify the tonic in non-contrastive utterances in RP as they did in dealing with ESE speech. However, just as in ESE speech, they readily identified contrasted items.

In the second and third of this set of experiments the judges were presented with a sub-set of twenty of the sentences from the first of these experiments. In each case the target sentence was embedded in three or four surrounding sentences. However they were presented under different conditions. In the second experiment the judges were simply asked to underline, on the written transcription, where they thought tonics would occur if the sentence was uttered. They did not hear a tape of the utterance. In the third of these experiments the judges were asked to perform the same task but this time they heard the tape of the utterance as well.*

The content of these experiments can be summarised thus (in each case of course the syntactic and lexical structure is the same):

1. Phonetic cues — no context
2. No phonetic cues — context
3. Phonetic cues — context

We wanted to know whether the tonic is indeed a phonological item which is identifiable by phonetic cues, as so much of the literature claims, or whether it is a complex construct which the listener identifies on the basis of information which he gleans from all types of source available to him — syntactic/semantic, contextual and phonetic.

We found that the spread of judgements in Experiments 1 and 2 was greater than in Experiment 3. In Experiment 1 the judges would select one locus in cases of clear contrastiveness. In other cases they selected at least two and, as in the earlier experiments, the phonetic cues of high pitch and maximum movement competed with the last lexical item. In Experiment 2, the judges tended to choose the last lexical item and, where the context clearly showed that an item in the target sentence was contrastive, they agreed in identifying that as a tonic. However there was a general tendency for judges to identify almost all potentially stressable items as tonics in this experiment. In Experiment 3, fewer items were chosen as tonics and there was a much stronger tendency for judges to agree with each other. These generalisations may be illustrated by the following sentence:

Was the old(AB) man(ABC) very well off

In Experiment 1, judges chose <u>old</u>, <u>man</u> and <u>off</u> as tonics. Here they are presumably influenced in their decisions by the height and movement(AB) on <u>old</u>, the height, movement and intensity(ABC) on <u>man</u> and the fact that <u>off</u> is the last stressed item. In 2, judges spread their votes between <u>old</u>, <u>man</u>, <u>very</u>, <u>well</u> and <u>off</u> with all of the judges

*At least a month elapsed between each of the experiments mentioned in this section. In the second and third of these experiments the target sentences were presented in a different order and intermixed with different sets of non-target utterances. For a detailed description of these experiments see Currie, forthcoming.

choosing at least two tonic loci. In 3, the judges chose only <u>man</u> and <u>off</u>. Here the context makes it clear that it is not the <u>oldness</u> of the man that is at issue but the whole constituent <u>old man</u>, and judges no longer identify <u>old</u> as tonic.

Conclusions

1. It seems clear from comparing the results of the first of these experiments with those described in 5.1. and 5.2. that judges find it no easier to identify tonics in RP than they do in ESE.

2. It seems clear that, where no item is phonetically identified as contrastive, judges are pulled in one direction by phonetic maxima (particularly pitch height) and in another by the last lexical item within a major syntactic constituent.

3. These experiments suggest, at least, that, except in cases of contrast, which are clearly phonetically marked, judges use all sorts of non-phonetic cues to identify an item which they call 'tonic'. Obviously, as we have seen consistently throughout these experiments, the last lexical item plays a very important part in this identification. It also seems very probable that the listener takes context into account in determining which phonetic cues to pay attention to. This view seems indicated by the results of the series of experiments discussed in this section. However, it is clear to us that more work needs to be done in this area, using a wider spread of data, before this can be asserted confidently.

5.4.   What is a Tonic?

We now have two separate sets of evidence which demonstrate considerable difficulty in identifying tonics, our own experience in attempting to describe conversational speech, which is reported in Chapter 3 and the experience of judges asked to identify tonics in an experimental situation which we have described in earlier sections of this chapter. We shall now enumerate some of the conclusions from work reported in these two areas which suggest to us that the notion of 'tonic' needs further refinement:

1. New lexical items are consistently introduced into conversation high in the speaker's pitch range, whereas given items are introduced lower in the speaker's pitch range (3.6.).

2. Some pause-defined units contain only lexical items which are treated by the speaker as given (3.6.).
3. Some pause-defined units contain more than one item which is treated by the speaker as new (3.6.).
4. In general, new items are introduced at or near the beginning of pause-defined units (often in thematic position in the clause) rather than at the end (3.6.). (Note that we state this only for the type of data described in this study. We would not wish to extend this claim to formal, goal-directed speech, since we have not studied this type of speech.)
5. In non-contrastive sentences, however short, judges, between them, identify at least two loci of prominence.
6. In non-contrastive sentences judges consistently tend to be divided between items which are marked by phonetic maxima early in the sentence and the last lexical item.

We suggest that the difficulties encountered by analysts trying to identify tonics in long stretches of language and by judges trying to identify tonics in short stretches of language arise from the same cause — that the notion of tonic as expounded, for instance, by Halliday and most other scholars, derives from two separate systems which may, quite frequently, cumulate on the same item but which very often fail to do so. We shall spend the rest of this section in attempting to justify this claim.

The system which has been consistently associated with the notion of tonic is the system of 'information structure' where information structure is taken to mean the marking by the speaker of what he assumes to be given ('recoverable anaphorically or situationally', Halliday, 1967) and of what he assumes to be new ('not in the sense that it cannot have been previously mentioned, although it is often the case that it has not been, but in the sense that the speaker presents it as not being recoverable from the preceding discourse', Halliday, 1967). Halliday claims, and many other scholars have made the same claim, that the tone group is the unit of organisation within which this given/new structure is to be perceived and that, in an unmarked utterance, the structure of information within the tone group will be such that given information precedes new information and that the focus of new information, hence the tonic, will fall on the last lexical item. Halliday also claims that a tone group must contain an obligatory new element, but only one, and that it may contain, optionally, a given element.

This account of information structure does not accord well with the sort of speech that we examined in Chapter 3, speech which is typical of our data. In this style of speech the speaker typically introduces a new item at the beginning of a unit, after a pause, and then tails away with a given structure which relates the new to the topic of discourse. So we find:

1. I regret + putting the people out of the out of the South Side and central Edinburgh you know
6. well the authority more or less made it that everybody was to go outside you know
8. I would reckon that eighty per cent of people
9. didnae want to go out of the town . . .
13. thirty years too late so to speak you know
14. that's what I regret . . .

In each case the new comes at the beginning of the unit and the speaker treats what follows as given. Since this is the normal pattern of information structure for our data it seems absurd to have to call all this, in Halliday's terms, 'marked' information structure. On the contrary, if Halliday is right in analysing the conversational speech of academics on which his framework is based as consisting of an unmarked given/new information structure, then we should claim that the sort of speech we are describing here is typologically distinct, in that it reveals a different principle of information structure.

We have to explain how it comes about that Halliday suggests that this given/new structure is indeed the norm, and why this notion of given/new structure has been so readily accepted by other scholars. In his most frequently referred-to article, Halliday (1967) first of all introduces the notion of 'information focus' and then begins a paragraph with the following observations: 'It was very early observed that in many, perhaps a majority of, instances in English the tonic falls on the last accented syllable in the tone group. This can be interpreted in the light of the phonological structure of the tone group, with obligatory tonic segment optionally preceded by a pretonic segment, to suggest the generalisation that the information unit consists of an obligatory new element, realised as tonic, optionally preceded by a given element, realised as pretonic.' Note that there is quite a jump in the argument here and the jump occurs in Halliday's interpretation of the word 'tonic'. Whereas other scholars have indeed noted that there are characteristic contours associated with the last stressed syllable (usually specified within a sentence) these scholars had not associated these contours with 'given and new structure', which is the jump that Halliday makes. We wish to claim that, whereas this insight of Halliday's has been enormously fruitful in opening up discussion of information structure in spoken language, one unfortunate by-product of the way he has formulated tonic function is that two distinct systems are conflated. The first is the given/new structure which Halliday is concerned to describe. The second is what Trubetzkoy (1969) calls a 'delimitative' system and what Pike (1945) calls a 'finality contour', i.e. a phonetic marker which marks the end of a syntactic/semantic unit.

Discussion of boundary markers in descriptions of British intonation has been curiously neglected. In the American structuralist tradition, where scholars were concerned with transcribing quantities of speech, the problem was fully recognised and led to many papers dealing with 'juncture' phenomena (see Trager and Smith, 1951). In the British tradition, which dealt largely with the description of short, constructed sentences cited out of context, the problem has rarely been faced. Halliday, as we pointed out in 3.1., is not concerned with the problem of demarcating tone group boundaries which is, in itself, surprising since he has contributed to the mass of papers working within the Firthian tradition of prosodic analysis (Halliday, 1959), a form of phonological analysis which is particularly concerned with the phenomena of boundary marking in language.* Crystal alone of British scholars has recognised the problem, necessarily, since he has worked at transcribing quantities of data, and has suggested the boundary criteria we discussed in 3.1. Even Crystal, however, does not suggest that the contour on the final accented syllable may itself constitute one of the boundary markers. Indeed he writes, 'it is the case that *after* this nuclear tone there will be a tone-unit boundary which is indicated by two phonetic factors . . . perceivable pitch change . . . very slight pause'. (Crystal, 1969, our emphasis.)

We suggest that in sentences read aloud there will generally be some extension of pitch movement on the last stressed syllable. This cannot be taken as marking new information since all items in the sentence must be new. What it does mark, we suggest, is 'sentence final'. Similarly, in texts read aloud, delimitative marking will regularly be heard, since the speaker is presented with a punctuated text, and what

*It was Mrs Eileen Whitley, one of the founding teachers of prosodic analysis, who pointed out to GB that many contours in English speech are 'equipollent' and utilise phonetic prominence in the first place as a marker of focus and in the second place as a marker of finality.

punctuation represents is delimitative marking. However, in
spontaneous speech we often find the end of a syntactic unit but no
corresponding phonological boundary marker. Thus, you will
remember, that in the text we discussed in 3.6., unit 9 consists of a
series of syntactic structures with no clear phonetically marked
boundaries:

> didnae want to go out of the town didnae want their gardens
> they were quite happy where they were if they'd built houses
> in the town

This unit is heard as a series of low stressed peaks bounded by two
higher peaks on <u>want</u> and <u>in</u>. We assume that the speaker does not
bother to mark the syntactic boundaries phonologically since
phonological delimitative markers are merely ancillary to the syntax,
as Trubetzkoy (1969) suggests: 'Each language possesses specific,
phonological means that signal the presence or absence of a
sentence . . . boundary at a specific point in the sound-continuum. But
these means are only ancillary devices. They can probably be compared
to traffic signals in the street. . . . It is possible to get along without
them: one need only be more careful and attentive. Therefore they are
not found on every street corner but only on some. Similarly, linguistic
delimitative elements generally do not occur in all positions concerned
but are found only now and then.' We should not be surprised, then, to
find sequences of syntactic structures where the speaker relies on the
syntax to do the signalling work. There may be occasions where the
speaker is making some point which demands clear syntactic chunking
(the distinction between restrictive and non-restrictive adjectives is, of
course, a traditional example of this, though not one that turns up in
our data). On these occasions the speaker may use phonological
delimitative markers to show how the sequence is to be structured. In
general the speaker is free to decide (except in topic-final structures)
whether or not he wishes to reinforce syntactic structure with
phonological boundary markers. In some styles of speech it may be the
case that the speaker regularly subdivides the pause-defined units into
syntactically structured units which are bounded by phonological
boundary markers. These boundary markers should be assumed to
include those intonation phenomena associated with the last stressed
syllable of a structure cited in isolation.

   In some styles of speech it may be the case that the boundary-
marking system does co-occur with new on the last lexical item — this

is certainly what Halliday's system suggests. However in our data this co-occurrence is rare. In general we find new lexis being introduced at the beginning of contours, on high pitch, and the last lexical item, which is usually given, is produced on a fairly low peak which falls to the base-line. The judges in our experiments are torn between these two points of prominence, the phonetic prominence associated with the new lexical item and the structural prominence (associated with some phonetic marking) of the last lexical item. The consistent pattern of identifying two loci of tonic within even two-word sentences suggests that the judges are trying to accommodate everything they have been told about the tonic: (i) that it marks new and (ii) in unmarked structures, will fall on the last lexical item. Their problem arises, we believe, because the term 'tonic' encompasses both given/new structure and final boundary marking.

We propose, therefore, at least for the description of conversational ESE, to withdraw from the view of information as structured in an unmarked given/new sequence within the tone group. In our data we can perceive no smooth progression of given (A)/new(B) information within one unit which is immediately followed in the next by a structure given(B)/new(C), where what is treated as new in the first unit is treated as given in the following unit. The speaker's organisation of his discourse is a good deal less patterned than this and involves keeping a lot of information in the air. We simply recognise that new (emphatic or contrastive, see discussion in 5.3.) items are generally introduced on high pitch and given items generally occur on low pitch. The hearer's judgement of what he has to treat as given and new will depend not only on pitch height but also what he knows about the context (see discussion in 5.3.). It follows that we do not specify an unmarked placing within a contour for the introduction of items the speaker wishes to treat as new. We cannot find a consistent pattern of introduction, except to say that new lexical items are introduced with high pitch. So in a constructed example which would, in Hallidaian terms, be held to exemplify 'marked tonicity' as in B:

A.   Who washed the car?
B.   Daddy washed (the car) (it)

we would expect to find washed and car introduced with high peaks in A, and Daddy introduced with a high peak in B, with washed and car dropped to lower peaks. In both cases we would expect to find car falling to the base-line and extended in duration, marking finality.

The discussion at this point has been restricted to new lexis — items introduced for the first time into a conversation. Halliday's account of what is treated by the speaker as new is a good deal more complex than this: ' "new" information is focal; not in the sense that it cannot have been previously mentioned, although it is often the case that it has not been, but in the sense that the speaker presents it as not being recoverable from the preceding discourse. The focal information may be a feature of mood, not of cognitive content . . . but this is still "new" in the sense intended.' (Halliday, 1967.) Later in the same paper he writes, 'The newness may lie in the speech function or it may be a matter of contrast with what has been said before or what might be expected.' We would certainly wish to follow Halliday in his account of the range of categories that the speaker may treat as new. In the extract from the speech of 22 BS discussed in 3.6. we noted examples of contrastive in, emphatic intonation focusing of the deictic that, and, in Chapter 6, we discuss a number of question-answer pairs where the answer reiterates the cognitive content of the question, as in A. Can you spell it B. Spell it? where B is puzzled at being asked to spell his name. The illocutionary function of these two utterances is clearly distinct, and it is this, we would suggest, that the speaker is treating as new here.

An aspect of information structure which is obscured in the treatment proposed here is the structuring of an information group around a focus. Halliday's 'unmarked' tone group structure, with the pretonic correlating with given and the tonic with new, reflecting the Prague school's notion of the communicative dynamism of a sentence which increases as the sentence progresses, depends on a notion of information structure within the tone group. This may be an appropriate analysis for information structure in written language or the conversations of academics, which tend to be syntactically more complex than the typically paratactic language of our data. In pause-defined units there may be several foci, marked as contrastive/emphatic or new by the speaker. The domain of focus may be partly specified by phonetic cues but, as the experiments described in 5.3. suggest, it is also specified by syntactic and contextual cues.

We assume that similar varieties (speech styles) of other accents of English will use intonation features in a similar way. However, we have not studied other accents in the same sort of detail and we do not know how the categories contrastive/new/given, which are generally marked in ESE by a progressive fall in pitch height, are marked in other accents. In particular we do not know how far the rather simple

pitch patterns that we appeal to in describing conversational ESE
would be adequate to describe, for example, the effect of the system of
tones that is recognised in RP. We assume that this system of tones has,
inter alia a boundary-marking function and an information-structure-
marking function.

APPENDIX A

Read/Speak Experiment

When anyone is asked to read a sentence they will often choose one word in the sentence as being the 'important' word. You are given a list of sentences on this page. We would like you to examine each sentence in turn; read each sentence *aloud*; select the word which you consider to be the most important word, and underline it; say the important word aloud, then read the sentence aloud once more.

1. How many children do you have?
2. He played squash on Mondays, Wednesdays, and Fridays.
3. There is my house.
4. How pleased they were when they heard it!
5. Three sons?
6. He lost each of the games they played.
7. Since the old man was a little deaf he always asked people to speak up.
8. The old man asked if she had posted the letter.
9. They missed the last bus so someone suggested taking a taxi.
10. Can I watch the game?
11. Have you change of a pound?
12. I have three daughters.
13. Do you want to play with me?
14. May I watch the game?
15. On Monday she got the gas bill, three days later she went to the bank, and on Friday she paid it.

APPENDIX B

Below is a short story. Read it through and try to remember it. Your partner will ask you questions about the events and characters in the story, but you should only answer yes or no. While you are being asked these questions, you may refer back to this typed copy.

How a Bad Daughter was made a Good Wife

Once there was a rich farmer who had three sons.

The eldest of them married a gentleman's daughter, who was very well off; and the second married a miller's daughter who was very beautiful. And the youngest of them, who was a carpenter, was then the only one of them left unmarried. He decided to marry.

'I'll get the daughter of a bad mother, as bad as I can find.'

He took his pony and his dog, and went away, not knowing how far he would go. The day was bad, and snow was falling. What did he see on his way but an old man at work ploughing in a field. He went over to him, and said:

'Oh, ho! you've got a bad day for ploughing.'

'Well,' said the old fellow, 'indeed, it isn't good.'

'Why do you have to work outside on a day like this?'

'If there was a way I could stay at home, I wouldn't come out myself; but I'd rather be outside, than indoors with the womenfolk. If her mother is bad, my daughter is seven times worse.'

'May I marry her?' asked the young man.

'I never saw anyone on whom I'd wish her, but if you think you can bring her to heel, I'll not keep her from you.'

'Oh, I'll take her right enough, if you'll give her to me.'

'That's just what I'll do,' said the old man.

So they agreed to get married; and the daughter of the old man became the wife of the farmer's youngest son. Then they left for his home. The pony was their only conveyance, and the girl was put behind him on the pony's back.

They left, and they hadn't gone far before the young husband's dog ran away. He shouted at the dog, but the dog paid no heed. When the dog did come back, he took a revolver out of his pocket and shot the dog and killed it.

'Goodness,' said his wife, 'why did you kill the dog?'

'Why should I let him live, a worthless creature that wouldn't listen to me?'

When they were getting near to his home, they came to a river which ran between them and the house. He put the pony at the worst bit of the stream, and began to lash the pony to make it go across the river. The pony only backed and would not go near it. He asked his wife to dismount, and he got off the pony himself, and took out his revolver, and put it to the pony, and killed it.

'My God, why did you kill the pony?' she said.

'Why should I let it live, a worthless creature that wouldn't do what I told it?'

He went and took the saddle off the pony.

'Here,' he said. 'You carry that.'

'Indeed I'll not carry it; you might have let the beast that was carrying it live; the saddle would be fitter on it than on me.'

'Are you saying you won't carry it?' he said.

'Oh, of course I'll carry it, but you really might have let the pony live, it would have been more suitable on her.'

'Well, if the pony had done what I told her, I wouldn't have killed her.'

They came home, he and she, and she was the best wife there had ever been! There was nothing he asked her to do that she wouldn't do!

APPENDIX C

This is a game of co-operation. Your partner has been given a story to read and remember. Below is a list of characters from the story (List A) and a list of actions or events from the story (List B). Your task is to match up List A and List B and reconstruct the story.

Your partner has already read the story. You may ask him/her questions about the story, but your partner may only answer yes or no. So you will not be able to ask questions like: Who had three sons? You may ask as many questions as you like until you think you know which characters performed which actions and in what order, that is, until you think you can tell the story. (Note: One character may perform *more* than one of the actions in List B.)

When you feel you are able, tell the whole story to your partner.

If you wish, you can make notes, draw connecting lines, or number actions on this sheet of paper.

List A (Characters)	List B (Actions/Attributes)
1. eldest son	a)_____ has a bad-natured wife and a daughter who is worse
2. youngest son	
3. old man	b)_____ does not obey command to return and is shot
4. miller's daughter	
5. bad-natured daughter	c)_____ had three sons
6. dog	d)_____ is impressed by previous events and becomes a very obedient wife
7. pony	
8. newly-married couple	
9. rich farmer	e)_____ returns home on the back of the pony
10. second son	
11. gentleman's daughter	f)_____ asks to marry bad-natured daughter
	g)_____ was very beautiful
	h)_____ went off with his pony and dog to look for the bad-natured daughter of a bad-natured mother

i)_____ refuses to cross a stream and is shot

j)_____ was very well off

k)_____ runs away

l) _____ married a gentleman's daughter

m)_____ decided to get married

n)_____ tells his wife to carry the saddle

o)_____ meets _____ ploughing a field in the snow

p)_____ married a miller's daughter

6.0. The Function of Tones

We have proceeded so far without confronting the area which many
scholars have seen as the most important area in intonation studies, that
of pitch-direction or 'tone'. Many of the best-known descriptions of
English intonation (notably those of Jones, 1962; Armstrong and Ward,
1929; O'Connor and Arnold, 1959 and Gimson, 1959, 1970) have been
primarily concerned with the description of systems of contrastive
tones, and their associated pre tonic contours, in RP. One reason why
we have been able to get so far in this description without paying
attention to tone must be clear from our transcription and the Fo
readings that we have presented: there is relatively little variation of
pitch direction on single syllables (or indeed on single words) in our
data. Nearly every stressed word is uttered on a fall in ESE.

There are very few examples of rise-falls and, when they do occur,
they carry none of the emotive overtones which are often associated
with them in descriptions of RP (see O'Connor and Arnold, 1959).
They tend to occur when the speaker has almost reached the base-line
at the end of a descending series of stressed items – one way available
to him, at this point, of stressing an item is to raise it up from the
base-line and let it fall again. We saw an example of this in the excerpt
produced by 22 BS (3.6., line 14): especially central south Edinburgh.
Here the stressed syllable of Edinburgh rises from 115 to 130 cps and
the following unstressed syllables then fall right down to 85 cps. This
seems to us perceptually equivalent to extending the duration of the
stressed syllable of a word uttered low in the speaker's tessitura. There
really seems to be no justification for considering it as a member of a
system of contrastive tones. We should perhaps point out yet again that
we have no examples of speakers behaving in a non co-operative way. It
could be that if we were to extend our data-base to include, for
example, instances of speakers being sarcastic, we should then
encounter a realisation of a genuine phonological rise-fall.

There are no examples of regular fall-rises in our ESE data either.
There are occasional instrumental recordings of dips in the middle of

stressed items but they tend to be associated with medial nasals. However, in our interactive dialogues especially, there is a number of examples where the speaker marks the end of a pause-defined unit by a fall-to-mid or a mid-level tone, as in the cases we discussed in 4.2. Rather more rarely, there are cases of the final stressed syllable bearing a rise-to-mid or even a rise-to-high. These are examples of rising tones on single syllables or words. How are we to account for these rises? Do they function in a different way from falls? In the rest of this chapter we shall examine these questions from a number of different points of view.

There is a well-established history of terminal-rising intonation being primarily associated with marking question function in descriptions of English. Thus Daniel Jones (1962) relates his tune 2 (rising intonation which, in his transcription, rises to just above the mid-line) to 'questions requiring the answer "yes" or "no"'. O'Connor and Arnold (1959) also relate rising intonation to questions; in their examples of tone group 8, which rises to high, utterances of all forms are marked with a question mark in final position. Gimson (1962) makes the same assumption: 'This nucleus, rising to a high pitch, is associated essentially with questions.' Quirk *et al.* (1972) suggest three criteria for identifying questions: 'a) the placing of the operator in front of the subject . . . b) the initial positioning of an interrogative or <u>wh</u> element . . . c) rising "question" intonation'. Halliday (1970) subscribes to the same view: 'We use a rising tone . . . in . . . the "yes/no" (or "general") question, where the uncertainty is precisely that between negative and positive.' The same position is assumed in many descriptions of American English (see discussion in Lieberman, 1967, Chapter 6, and Uldall, 1964).

Alongside this view of a 'question intonation' there has also existed the view that no particular intonation pattern can regularly be associated with a particular speech function. In general it is those who have spent time analysing sequential speech rather than citation sentences who have held this view. Thus Pike (1945) writes:

> Popular nonlinguistic tradition would seem to claim that there is a question pitch as distinct from a statement pitch; all questions are presumed to use the first of these two, and, as a corollary, the question pitch would not occur on statements. The evidence fails to support the assumption. There are many more contours than one for question and one for statement. Specifically, it was a marked surprise to me to find that there are many different contours which can be used on questions . . . and that for any contour used on a

question I could usually find the same one used on a statement;
likewise for all, or nearly all, contours used on statements, I found
the same ones used on questions . . . In other words, there appeared
to be no question intonation as such.

Others who have taken a similar view include Hultzen (1959), Fries
(1964), Bolinger (1965), Crystal (1969) and Gunter (1972).

   The British scholars whose views we have cited were working with
RP and the American scholars with 'General American'. It seemed to
us worthwhile to examine this problem in the comparatively untrodden
field of Scottish intonation. We approached the problem from two
points of view. First we wanted to determine whether or not, for the
general public, there does exist a stereotype notion of 'question
intonation'. Secondly we examined a corpus of questions occurring
in our data to see whether they were regularly associated with a
particular terminal tone.

6.1. Intonation Stereotypes and the Effect of Context

Our first problem was the delimitation of the term 'question'. This is a
problem which has been discussed by scholars primarily interested in
the linguistic correlates of question function (notably Bolinger, 1958)
and also by sociolinguists interested in the sociological function of
questions (see Hymes, 1974; Goody, 1978) as well as by linguistic
philosophers within the theory of speech acts (notably by Searle,
1969). We were not able to rely on formal linguistic markers in our
investigation since what we were trying to do was establish the function
of one of these recognised formal markers, rising intonation. We did not
have access to the minds of the speakers on our tapes to find out what
they knew or what they thought their interlocutors knew when they
asked a particular question. We were forced to adopt a simple heuristic
which is almost as leaky as the notion 'question'. When what we
thought was a question was answered by the next speaker by 'yes/no'
or by filling in a questioned slot in a WH question, we identified the
first member of this 'adjacency pair' as indeed a question. There were
other types of item which are a good deal more tricky. Consider the
following dialogue:

1. A.   and have you lived in Edinburgh all your life
2. B.   yes

3. A.   have you moved around at all
4. B.   travelling

The pair 1 and 2 form a straightforward question-answer pair, 3 and
4 are obviously less straightforward. In 3, A asks what is formally
marked as a question (and is situationally also marked since this
sequence occurs at the very beginning of one of the interviews where
the role of A is quite clearly established as question-asker). What is the
status of 4? We take this to be a counter-question by B of a sort we
term 'interpretive', where speaker A uses a term which speaker B is not
sure how to interpret, so B offers some other term, which A then
accepts or rejects. This is what happens in the sequence here where A
reformulates question 3. We rely, then, on the notion of adjacency
pair (as discussed, for example, in Garfinkel, 1970) to identify
questions.

None of the questions which we discuss in this chapter arose from
the game situation which we describe in 5.2. We wanted to avoid the
criticisms levelled against the methodology of Fries (1964), who made
general claims for the intonation of polar questions based exclusively
on panel-game data. The questions we discuss here arise naturally
during spontaneous conversation.

We abstracted twenty-five short utterances from conversations
between Karen Currie and ESE speakers. The utterances were between
one and three words long. Five of these utterances were answers to
questions, the rest were what we judge to be questions of various sorts.
None of the utterances is syntactically marked for mood.

These utterances were presented to judges under two different
conditions. In the first condition, judges heard each isolated utterance
three times, with an 8-second interval, and were asked simply to judge
whether the utterance was or was not a question by ticking one of two
boxes. (The format of presentation appears at the end of this chapter.)
In the second condition judges were presented with the same taped
utterances but this time the utterances were embedded in the
immediately preceding and following context of discourse. In this
presentation subjects had a written transcript of the relevant chunk of
text with the short utterance they were to pay attention to underlined.
Once again they were asked to judge whether or not the part
underlined was or was not a question. (The format of this presentation
appears at the end of this chapter.)

The judges were grouped into two different sets. They were final-
year students in secondary school. They encountered the texts in

small groups of five or six with both Karen Currie and Joanne Kenworthy present, to make it clear that this was a serious enterprise. The first, decontextualised, set of utterances was presented to 19 judges, the second to 22 judges.

6.1.i Decontextualised Utterances

What we wanted to know was whether the judges operated with a stereotype of question intonation which would enable them to make confident judgements about whether an isolated utterance was a question or not a question. We intended to look particularly at rising intonation and placing high in the speaker's tessitura to see whether these cues function (as has been claimed for instance by Hadding-Koch and Studdert-Kennedy, 1964) as markers of question function. Figure 6.1 shows the impressionistic transcription of the intonation of the 25 utterances. Table 6.1 shows the judgements for the two experiments.

Of the 25 short utterances, four have unequivocal terminal rises-to-high, numbers 3, 8, 17 and 19. Of these four utterances, three (8, 17 and 19) are identified by at least 16 judges as questions. Number 3, however, which has a pattern very like that in 17, splits the judges in half and only nine judge it as a question. It might be supposed that this results from the experimental design and that the judges were predisposed, to begin with, to expect items not to be questions. However, it is worth looking across to the results of the next experiment, where judges have access to context as well as the utterance, where item 3 is now judged by 21 out of 22 judges not to be a question whereas all the other three items are judged by at least 17 judges to be questions.

A further three utterances (6, 7 and 13) also have terminal rises, but rises-to-mid. Of these, 17 judges judge 7 to be not-a-question, 14 judge 13 to be not-a-question and judges are evenly split on 6.

Eight utterances involve a fall to well below the mid-line (2, 9, 10, 11, 14, 22, 24 and 25). Four of these (10, 11, 22 and 25) have at least 17 judges saying they are not questions but 14, which has a contour very like that of 10, is judged by 18 judges to be a question. The remaining three of this set (2, 9 and 24) split the judges fairly evenly — notably 24 which reaches very low at the end of the fall.

We can find no patterning of onset pitch which relates to the choices made by the judges.

In 17 out of the 25 utterances more than 75 per cent of the judges agreed on the assignment. Eight utterances yielded less clear results

Figure 6.1

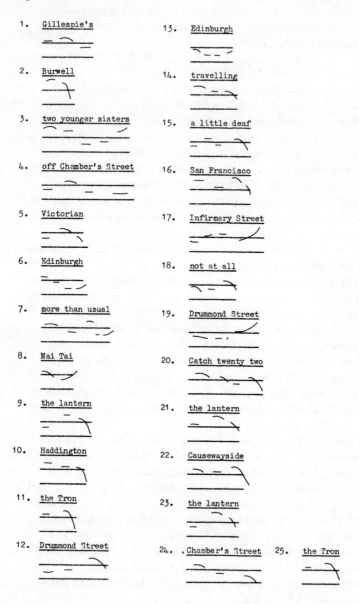

Table 6.1: Question or Not-a-Question Experiment

	Contextualised utterance (listening)		Decontextualised utterance (listening)	
	Question	Not Qu.	Question	Not Qu.
1.	0	22	1	18
2.	19	3	6	13
3.	1	21	9	10
4.	12	10	4	15
5.	14	8	0	19
6.	0	22	9	10
7.	1	21	2	17
8.	17	5	19	0
9.	21	1	10	9
10.	1	21	1	18
11.	3	19	1	18
12.	17	5	16	3
13.	16	6	5	14
14.	22	0	18	1
15.	11	11	3	16
16.	22	0	18	1
17.	22	0	16	3
18.	21	1	12	7
19.	22	0	18	1
20.	0	22	0	19
21.	22	0	11	8
22.	6	16	2	17
23.	22	0	15	4
24.	7	15	9	10
25.	6	16	2	17

(2, 3, 6, 9, 13, 18, 21 and 24).

Of the 17 items where 75 per cent of judges agreed on the assignment, seven of these are judged to be questions (8, 12, 14, 16, 17, 19 and 23). We have already noted that 8, 17 and 19 are characterised by terminal high rises. Both 12 and 16 show final falls from quite high to mid. (So does 21 which, however, is judged a question only by a narrow majority on the first presentation.) This leaves 14 and 23, both of which show falls from quite high to just below the mid-line. (On the other hand so does 2 which judges in this decontextualised presentation judge by 13-6 to be not-a-question, though in the next contextualised presentation the judgement for this item is 19-3 in favour of question.)

6.1.ii The Utterances Contextualised

In this presentation the judges heard the same utterances. This time the immediately preceding and following utterances surrounded the extract, which was underlined in the written transcript. Twenty-two judges took part in this assignment.

In 18 out of the 25 utterances more than 75 per cent of the judges now agree on the assignment. There are some dramatic differences between the assignments made with the addition of context. The most dramatic differences come in the group which yielded ambivalent results in the first experiment (numbers 2, 3, 6, 9, 13, 18, 21 and 24). In six of these cases, where the judges were split in the decontextualised experiment, we now find 19 or more judges agreeing on the assignment for utterances 2, 3, 6, 9, 18 and 21 and the remaining two cases show a much clearer assignment, a 2/3 to 1/3 split.

Among the 17 utterances where a majority of more than 75 per cent of judges agree in the first assignment, six yield judgements showing more disagreement now that context is provided (4, 5, 8, 15, 22 and 25). This muddying effect of context is particularly clear in cases 5 and 8, both of which attracted 19-0 judgements in the first presentation. In 5, Victorian has a clear fall which is judged to be not-a-question in the first presentation. The context is not particularly helpful in this case. It seems to be a reflective repetition by the speaker of what the previous speaker has just said. Nothing signals it as a question to us but obviously some of our judges felt that it was not obviously functioning as not-a-question. In 8, the majority of speakers still believe that Mai Tai has some sort of question function but five judges do not and indeed it is by no means clear what the function of this utterance is in this context. The ambivalent effect of context in these cases appears to disturb the confident judgements the judges made on the basis of phonetic stereotypes.

The items which are judged by more than 75 per cent of judges to be questions on this presentation, include items 2, 8, 9, 12, 14, 16, 17, 18, 19, 21 and 23. This set can be characterised as all containing (i) terminal rise-to-high (8, 17 and 19) or (ii) high pitch followed by fall-to-mid (12, 16, 21 and 23) or (iii) high pitch followed by a fall-to-low (2, 9, 14 and, rather dubiously, 18). There are, of course, items which are judged by a majority of judges to be not-questions which share these characteristics. All we can say on the basis of this data is that there does seem to be a tendency for question function to be associated with high pitch.

In general, then, the effect of context is most marked among the set of assignments where there was most disagreement between judges in the first presentation. As we have seen, in most of these cases, context provides clues which the judges make obvious use of in making their assignments.

Conclusions

1. There is a tendency for judges to judge items in isolation with a terminal rise-to-high as questions (8, 17 and 19 but not 3).

2. Judges are more likely to judge items to be not-questions when they are cited in isolation than when they are cited in context (56 per cent of 475 judgements in the first presentation, 45 per cent of 550 judgements in the second presentation).

3. Context does have an effect on judges' decisions and, in general, tends to lead to greater agreement. In some cases, however, judges find it much harder to judge what is or is not a question when they are presented with an item in context. It seems likely that what affects judgements here is the fact that the notion 'question' is not clearly defined.

4. We can see no consistent intonational cue to what is or is not a question. We are rather surprised that our judges agree as much as they do on the utterances cited out of context. Experimentation in this area is clearly necessary. We need to know how well judges would perform on test-retest where they hear the same data on a different occasion. We need to offer judges much larger samples of utterances exhibiting different intonational features – height as against rise-to-high, as against rise-to-mid, etc. We need to offer judges longer extracts which do contain indications of mood, in order to see what the effect of the interaction of syntactic structure and intonation is. We need to use material which is functionally constrained in terms of being either first member or second member of adjacency pairs. We also need to ask questions other than 'is this a question or not a question?': an obvious candidate would be 'is this the last utterance on this topic or is there more to come?'.

6.2. Questions in ESE Data

We examined a sample of 200 questions (identified by the criteria we discussed in 6.1.) freely produced by subjects in the course of conversation or during the administration of the questionnaire. We examined them in terms of three parameters: (i) syntactic form,

(ii) terminal tone and (iii) context in which they occur. We were
particularly interested to see whether a given syntactic form is regularly
associated with a given tone as so much of the literature suggests. In
particular we wanted to see whether 'yes/no' questions would regularly
be associated with terminal rise-to-high. When we found examples of
particular syntactic forms which did not co-occur with the predicted
intonation pattern, we turned to the context of the utterance to see
whether it was possible to abstract any generalisations deriving from
context which would account for the variety of form.

6.2.i   Polar Questions

Polar questions, yes/no questions, are formed by positioning 'the
operator in front of the subject' (Quirk *et al.*, 1972). We found 36 of
these in our 200 questions. Of these 36, eight were produced with a
terminal rise, e.g.:

1.

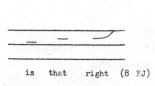

is   that   right (8 EJ)

(EJ has been presented with the photograph of old Edinburgh and
asked to determine where it was taken from. She looks at it and says
Well+ it's in Edinburgh and it's just down off the Grassmarket I would
say ++ before you go down into the Grassmarket + is that right.)

2.

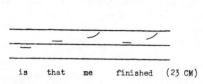

is   that   me   finished (23 CM)

(CM has completed the questionnaire and text reading and has been
chatting to KC about her holidays. When she has finished talking about
this she looks expectantly at KC and asks this question.)

Fourteen polar questions were produced with a fall-to-mid:

3.

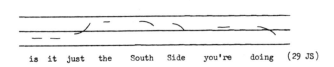

is it just the South Side you're doing (29 JS)

(The interview has apparently been concluded and KC has said thank
you very much and at this point JS begins to ask about the point of the
project.)

4.

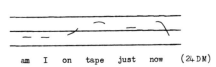

am I on tape just now (24 DM)

(DM is about to give the names of other possible informants. He wants
to know whether the tape recorder is still running because if it is, it
will not be necessary to write down these names.)

5.

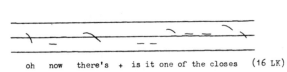

oh now there's + is it one of the closes (16 LK)

(LK is looking at the photograph and trying to identify where it is
taken from.)

A further fourteen polar questions are produced with a final fall-to-
low:

6.

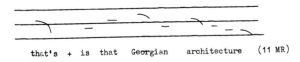

that's + is that Georgian architecture (11 MR)

(MR has been looking at the photograph and has correctly identified
the point it was taken from. She now points to a building in the
photograph and asks this question.)

7.

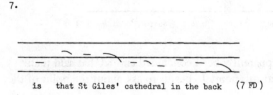

is   that St Giles' cathedral in the back   (7 FD)

(FD is looking at the photograph. As she speaks she points to the
tower of St Giles half-hidden at the back of the photograph.)

8.

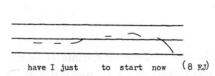

have I just   to start now   (8 EJ)

(At the beginning of the interview EJ was told that she would be asked
a few questions and then asked to read a short text aloud. When the
questionnaire section is completed KC asks EJ if she would read the
text. EJ picks it up, starts reading the title, checks herself and turns to
KC and asks the question.)

These questions are grouped together into three sets on the basis of
their final pattern: terminal rise-to-high, terminal fall-to-mid, terminal
fall-to-low. It is clear, to begin with, that the same syntactic structure
can occur with these three types of intonation pattern. Does the
context of utterance provide us with information which would enable
us to predict that one tone would be used in a given context rather
than another?

First, consider the last set, 6 to 8, those which have a terminal
fall-to-low. In all three cases it seems plausible to suggest that the
speaker is fairly confident of the answer to the question, and is simply
using the question to check the correctness of his/her assumption.
They are conducive questions in which the speaker is expecting the
answer 'yes'. There is some evidence to support this suggestion. In 6,
the speaker begins with a that's which would presumably introduce a
statement, but then switches to an interrogative. In 7, the speaker

speaks confidently in identifying the building as St Giles' cathedral, which is reasonable enough since this is the only building in Edinburgh topped by the very distinctive 'crown of thorns' lantern. In 8, the speaker has already demonstrated her assumption that she is to begin reading by beginning to read. It seems clear that she is simply checking that she is performing correctly. Bolinger (1958) comes to very similar conclusions in his examination of questions in American English.

The question then, is whether or not the other sets of questions (1-2, 3-5) are also conducive. Hudson (1975) suggests a sincerity condition on all polar interrogatives: 'All polar interrogatives seem to be subject to a sincerity condition, to the effect that the speaker believes that the hearer knows, at least as reliably as the speaker does, whether the proposition is true or false. This of course explains why speakers ask "ordinary" polar interrogatives: they don't know themselves whether the proposition is true but they think the hearer will or may.' It is quite clear that the speaker, in all our examples, must assume that KC does know whether the proposition is true or false, since KC is in control of the interview. The point to stress here is that what matters is not whether the speaker believes that the hearer knows the answer, since the speaker must believe that the hearer knows, but whether there are differences in the degree of commitment of the speaker to the truth of the proposition he expresses. Whereas in the set with terminal fall-to-low the speaker is almost certain that his proposition is true, in the sets 1-2, 3-5 he is less confident that he is right. In 3, for instance, the speaker has no evidence either way; all he knows is that he has been selected because he comes from the South Side. In 4, again, the speaker does not know whether or not the tape recorder is switched on. This is an open question. In 5, the speaker speaks slowly and tentatively and goes on to say she really has no idea where the photograph is taken from. (It is not taken from one of the closes.) These three utterances, then, do not appear to express any expectation on the part of the speaker of expecting the answer 'yes' rather than 'no'.

How do the first two utterances differ from 3-5? They appear to be, just like 3-5, quite open questions in which the speaker really does not know what the correct answer is. Hudson suggests that 'rising intonation would show that the speaker DEFERS to the hearer with respect to the truth of the proposition'. This certainly seems to hold true for 1-2 but it is hard to see that it is not also true for utterances 3-5.

To summarise: polar questions may be asked (i) with terminal rise-to-

high, (ii) with terminal fall-to-mid, (iii) with terminal fall-to-low. In the
case of both (i) and (ii) (both not-low terminations) the questions are
non-conducive — that is to say, the speaker has no expectation of one
answer being more likely than the other. In the case of (iii) the speaker
is asking a conducive question and clearly expects one answer rather
than the other.

6.2.ii   Declarative Questions

It has often been claimed in the literature that when there is no
syntactic marking of interrogative, an utterance may be produced with
a terminal rise-to-high and this rise will mark it as having question
function. Thus 'The declarative question is a type of question which is
identical in form to a statement, except for the final rising question
intonation . . . Declarative questions have "positive orientation" (or
"negative orientation") . . . They are similar in force to . . . tag
questions, except for a rather casual tone, which suggests that the
speaker takes the answer <u>yes</u> (or <u>no</u>) as a foregone conclusion.' (Quirk
et al., 1972.) We find many examples of declarative questions in our
data. However none of them has rising intonation. They all terminate
with fall-to-low, as in the following examples:

9.

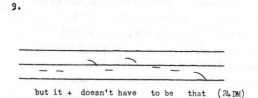

but it + doesn't have   to be   that   (24 DM)

(DM has asked KC whether it is important for the survey to have equal
numbers of male and female subjects. KC replies, we'd like a spread.
DM then produces this utterance to which KC replies, no, not really.)

10.

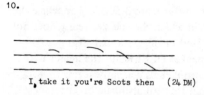

I take it you're Scots then   (24 DM)

(DM has been talking to KC about what characterises the Scottish
accent. JK, who has hitherto been silent, remarks that when travelling

abroad one can instantly recognise a Scottish voice. DM then utters 10.
JK replies, No, can you guess what I am? I'm very difficult, people are
very confused about me.)

11.

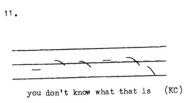

you don't know what that is   (KC)

(DM has been shown the photograph of Edinburgh. DM says, I just
can't figure out which angle you're on at all. KC points to a dome in
the photograph and asks 11. DM replies No.)

  In these examples the interlocutor in each case responds either
affirmatively or negatively. This indicates that the interlocutor
interpreted the utterance as a question requiring an answer yes or no in
spite of there being no formal marker, syntactic or intonational, of
question function. How is it that a participant in a conversation
recognises that a question is being asked when an utterance is not
formally marked as being a question? It may of course simply be the
case that the distinction question/statement is by no means as clear as is
often suggested. The speakers here are producing what could be
functionally called 'try-statements,* trying out a hypothesis in the
expectation that they are correct but, obviously, knowing that they are
making a statement about what their interlocutor knows, which always
risks a contradiction. When the interlocutor recognises that a statement
has been made about his domain of knowledge, he feels free to accept
or contradict it. He treats it as though it were a question. The crucial
point at issue here appears to be who it is that is accepted by the
participants as the repository of the relevant knowledge.

  These items, called 'declarative questions' (in spite of their being
uttered on a fall-to-low) are, as in the polar fall-to-low questions,
obviously conducive.

---

*See Keenan and Schieffelin (1976) who propose the term 'try marker' for
utterances marked by using intonation or interrogative structure which a speaker
uses to check if a referent is identified by the hearer (e.g. You can see X over
there?).

6.2.iii   *WH-Questions*

Like the declarative questions, WH-questions display a narrow range of contours.

In descriptions of RP, WH-questions are usually said to be associated with a fall. The following are typical representations:

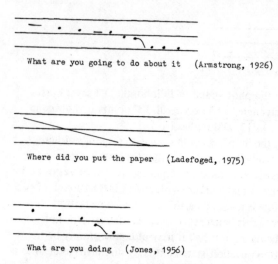

What are you going to do about it   (Armstrong, 1926)

Where did you put the paper   (Ladefoged, 1975)

What are you doing   (Jones, 1956)

In describing the pitch of WH-questions, Armstrong remarks, 'The pitch of final unstressed syllables is most important. These must be either on a low level, which is most usual, or, must begin with a very low and descend a little lower.' This is, of course, consistent with the description of RP as an accent with an inclined base-line where final, unstressed syllables will appear low in the speaker's tessitura. In ESE, WH-questions do not end low in the speaker's tessitura but at about the level established for Set B (3.6.iv) unstressed syllables in the earlier part of the utterance. Daniel Jones (1956) noted this feature of Scottish intonation in WH-questions: 'Often in Scotland the final stressed syllable of a sentence has a very high pitch with a very slight fall.' Here are some examples from our data:

11.

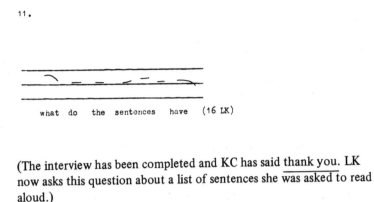

what do   the sentences   have   (16 LK)

(The interview has been completed and KC has said thank you. LK now asks this question about a list of sentences she was asked to read aloud.)

12.

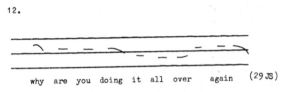

why are you doing it all over   again   (29 JS)

(JS is in the middle of reading the list of sentences. Some of them resemble each other very closely. She interrupts in the middle of the list to ask this question.)

13.

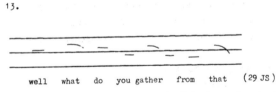

well   what   do   you gather   from   that   (29 JS)

(JS asks this question at the end of the interview just after KC has thanked her for participating.)

14.

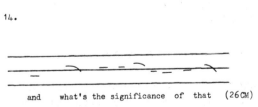

and   what's the significance of that   (26 CM)

(CM asks this question at the end of the questionnaire section of the inteview.)

15.

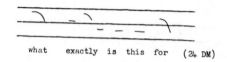

what   exactly is this for   (24 DM)

(DM asks this question after she has finished reading the sentences.)

A very consistent pattern is associated with these WH-questions. The WH-word is boosted on to a high peak and the final stressed word is again boosted on to a high peak – yielding an equal-peaked contour. Stressed items between these two main peaks may be boosted in pitch but are not realised so high as the initial and final peaks. Both peaks fall typically to the Set B unstressed syllable level – to mid.

6.2.iv   Echo Questions

Echo questions are questions in which the speaker repeats all or part of the preceding utterance of his interlocutor. They are usually treated separately from other question types in intonation studies and said to be uttered on a rising intonation (Jones, 1956; Kingdon, 1958).

It seems possible to distinguish between two main types of echo questions, questions where the speaker is questioning the appropriateness of whatever was said in the previous utterance, and questions where the speaker did not hear/understand some part of the previous utterance. Consider these two short constructed dialogues:

1. A.   How many people were there?
   B.   Oh, about fifty I guess.
   A.   Fifty?
   B.   Yes, quite a good number for a Monday night.
2. A.   How many people were there?
   B.   Oh, about fifty I guess.
   A.   How many?
   B.   Fifty, quite a good number for a Monday night.

In 1, A questions the appropriateness of the number fifty. (This could be spoken, of course, in a variety of ways, ranging from an expression of incredulity to a mere check for confirmation.) In 2, A requires a repetition of the number (either because he has not heard it or because he finds it difficult to believe). In 1 the speaker heard everything that was said. His <u>fifty</u> then is conducive, and we will expect a fall-to-low (unless he is expressing some strong attitude like incredulity). In 2 A did not hear what was being said, so his utterance cannot be conducive, so we will expect a rise-to-high or a fall-to-mid.

Examples of type 1 in our data include:

16.

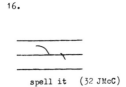

spell it   (32 JMcC)

(JMcC is clearly puzzled at KC's request to spell a very common surname and 'checks' that she has heard correctly.)

17.

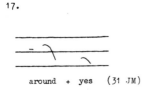

around + yes   (31 JM)

(JM utters this in response to the question <u>Have you moved around at all</u> and seems unclear how to interpret the question. After this <u>around + yes</u> KC expands on what the question means.)

The problem is, what is to count as a question. The effect of this type of utterance by the speaker, an echo of some part of his interlocutor's utterance but with no further development of it, seems always to be to provoke the first speaker into expansion or explanation of what he says. If utterances of this kind are included as 'questions', as by the criteria discussed in 6.1. they must be, since they are responded to by the interlocutor, we arrive at a definition of question that looks like this: *a short utterance which provokes a response on the same topic by the interlocutor.*

There are many examples of echo questions where the speaker did not hear, or believed he had not heard, a word in the previous utterance. These were acquired by the expedient of saying to subjects when they first saw the photograph of old Edinburgh, <u>Do you recognise the lantern?</u> ('Lantern' is an architectural term which is applied to the 'crown of thorns' structure on the tower of St Giles' cathedral.) Most of the subjects were unfamiliar with this term. Thus there are many responses like the following to the question <u>Do you recognise the lantern?</u>:

18.

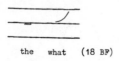

the   what   (18 BF)

19.

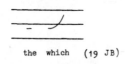

the   which   (19 JB)

The same pattern recurs in

20.

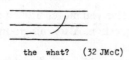

the   what?   (32 JMcC)

in response to <u>tell me about the South Side.</u>

These questions are non-conducive since the speaker does not think he has heard what was said. Here is the familiar pattern of rise-to-high or fall-to-mid which we associated with non-conduciveness in polar questions.

Conclusions

1. Three different terminal tones occur on the questions in our sample of ESE speech – rise-to-high (A), fall-to-mid (B), fall-to-low (C).

They are distributed in the following manner among the question types:

polar questions	A	B	C
declarative questions			C
WH-questions		B	
echo questions	A	B	C

2. The terminals appear to relate in a consistent way to the conduciveness of the question. Where the questions appear to be non-conducive, as in some polar questions, all WH-questions and some echo-questions, the terminal is either A or B. We can find no regular feature in our data to account for the appearance of A rather than B and have to conclude that they are in free variation. Conducive questions, all declarative questions and some polar questions, are regularly asked on a fall-to-low, C.

6.3. The Intonation of Questions

A number of recent studies have looked closely at the role of high rising intonation and intonation placed high in the pitch range with particular reference to the speech of young children. Thus, Garnica (1977) writes: 'Rising final terminals . . . may serve a social function — to regulate conversation between adult and child . . . rising terminals may cue the child as to when he is expected to respond.' Brown and Levinson (1978) point out that utterances produced high in the pitch range are associated with children, and are frequently reverted to by adults to demonstrate that they are vulnerable or being tentative or being deferent to their interlocutor. There is now plenty of evidence to show that very young children are frequently addressed using polar questions with high rising intonation — marking both syntactically and intonationally that the child should respond. Goody (1978) suggests that parents actively train the child to participate in conversations by cueing them in this way when it is their turn to speak.

It seems likely that rise-to-high terminal tone can be related to at least three distinct systems:

1. Cueing to continue on the same topic. If the speaker gives up his turn with a final rise-to-high, he demands that the next speaker continue on the same topic. If he utters a rise-to-high himself and does not give away his turn, he himself will continue on the same topic. (It is obviously one of the functions of a rhetorical question in formal speech to focus on the topic and mark that more is to come on this same topic.)

2. If the speaker is unsure of the truth of a proposition he may produce
an utterance with a final rise-to-high (or placed high in the pitch
range) thus marking a non-conducive utterance. A co-operative
interlocutor will then confirm or deny the proposition expressed in
this utterance — again maintaining the topic.

3. If the speaker feels deferent to his interlocutor he may mark the
final giving-away utterance of his turn by a rise-to-high, together
with a 'deferential' soft voice quality, perhaps smiling, etc. Again
the expectation must be that a co-operative interlocutor will
continue with the topic broached in the speaker's last utterance.

Any or all of these may constitute the reason for a speaker choosing
to use a rise-to-high tone. It does not seem possible to relate this too
closely to speakers needing information and believing that the interlocutor
has this information, since this is surely a property of all questions.
Only a tiny minority of questions to adults are uttered with rise-to-high.
A speaker must choose a high rise for a particular reason since this does
not constitute a normal choice. We believe that the interaction of the
three systems listed here is principally responsible for this choice.

6.4. The Tones of Core ESE

The domain of tonal contrast in ESE is identified as the last stressed
syllable of a pause-defined unit (with any following unstressed syllables
continuing in the direction established in the last stressed syllable).
Stressed syllables which occur before the last stressed syllable in a
pause-defined unit regularly fall towards the base-line.

It has already been suggested (5.4.) that two systems may cumulate
on the last stressed syllable: (i) the information-value marking system
(which will assign boosted peaks to contrastive/emphatic items, peaks
to new items and depressed peaks to given items) and (ii) the
delimitative system whose function it is to mark the boundaries of
items which must be co-interpreted.* We now suggest that the
unmarked realisation of the delimitative system will yield a fall-to-low.
(In the excerpt produced by 22 BS in 3.6., he regularly fell back to the
base-line at the end of each pause-defined unit.) The amount of fall-to-
low, whether the fall is from high or mid or is, indeed, realised as an
almost level-low, is determined by the information-value marking
system. (It may also be influenced by affective meaning or attitude.)

---

*The delimitative system is not only realised on the last stressed item of a pause-
defined unit, as we pointed out in 5.4., but may also be realised on final stressed
items of syntactic units within a pause-defined unit. Clearly the last stressed item
must necessarily be classified in terms of contrastive/new/given.

How then are we to treat the remaining tones that we have identified as occurring within the same domain, the rise-to-high, the rise-to-mid, the fall-to-mid and the mid-level? Any tone involving a relatively high peak or boosted peak (rise-to-high, fall-to-mid) is realising the information-value system and is marking an item as contrastive/emphatic or new. All these tones with not-low terminals are markers of non-conduciveness in questions. In utterances which are not questions, they are markers of the speaker's intention that the same topic shall be continued (either by himself or by the next speaker) – the 'more to come' marking. Note that the speaker is not obliged to mark more to come intonationally. He may choose to do it with incomplete syntax as 22 BS did, or by more formal syntactic marking, like subordination. If he is in danger of losing his turn, and produces a complete syntactic structure, he is more likely to mark his intended continuation by a not-low terminal. Other considerations, like tentativeness or deference, may influence a speaker to choose a rising tone rather than the normal falling tone.

These suggestions are summarised in Figure 6.2. All tones on final stressed syllables in pause-defined units are delimitative markers – this is not a contrastive function as Trubetzkoy's discussion, cited earlier, makes clear, and therefore does not appear in this matrix. All tones necessarily realise the system of information-value, and all contrast/ emphasis items are treated by the speaker as new. In the context of questions, tones which do not fall to low mark the question as non-conducive. The last two columns represent options open to the speaker – the marking of more to come and the marking of attitude (deference, etc.).*

The matrix in Figure 6.2 makes it clear which tones must be regarded as contrastive on the basis of their function. Low and not-low terminals must be distinguished on the basis of their discriminatory function in conducive/non-conducive questions and positively marking continuation of the topic. The value of distinguishing between fall-to-mid and rise is much less clear and appears to rest on attitudinal differences, but what these are, and how they combine with other features of intonation, voice quality, illocutionary force, context of situation etc, we cannot yet state. We distinguish, then, between low and not-low terminals. Similarly we distinguish between peaks, boosted peaks and depressed peaks. Figure 6.3 shows the major distinctions.

*Naturally other tones than rises, in combination with other paralinguistic features, also mark attitude – and, obviously, rises do not always necessarily mark deference; a sequence of rises-to-high combined with extended tessitura, loudness and a 'harsh' voice quality may, on the contrary, sound hectoring.

In boxes C and D the fundamental distinction between low and not-low terminals is represented. In A and B these are shown boosted, and E and F depressed. In boxes B, D, E and F, where two phonetically distinct pitch shapes are characterised, these are, as far as we can tell, in free variation with each other.

The tones of the core intonation pattern of ESE can be described in terms of three relative pitch heights distributed on the final stressed syllables of pause-defined units, and two terminals, low and not-low.

Figure 6.2: Functions Related to Tone-types

		New	Contrast/ Emphasis	Conducive (Questions)	Continues Topic	Defer- ence/etc.
Fall- to- Low	from boost	+	+	+		
	peak	+	−	+		
	mid	−	−	+		
	low-level	−	−	+		
Fall- to- Mid	from boost	+	+	−	+	
	peak	+	−	−	+	
	mid-level	−	−	−	+	
Rise	to boost	+	+	−	+	+
	peak	+	−	−	+	+
	mid	−	−	−	+	+

Figure 6.3: Phonetic Realisation of Tones

	Low Terminal	Not-low Terminal
Boost	A boost-high-fall-to-low	B boost-high-fall-to-mid rise-to-boost-high
Peak	C high-fall-to-low	D high-fall-to-mid rise-to-high
Depress	E mid-fall-to-low low-level	F mid-level rise-to-mid

APPENDIX A

You will hear 25 utterances, all of them one to three words long, which
have been taken from taped conversations. Some of them are questions,
some are answers to questions, exclamations, statements, etc. We would
like you to try and decide *which are questions*. You will hear each
utterance three times. Before each playing you will hear a warning
bleep. If you think the utterance is a question, tick the box 'Question',
if you think the utterance is not a question, tick the box 'Not-Question'.

		Question	Not-Question
1.	Gillespie's		
2.	Burwell		
3.	two younger sisters		
4.	off Chambers Street		
5.	Victorian		
6.	Edinburgh		
7.	more than usual		
8.	Mai Tai		
9.	the lantern		
10.	Haddington		
11.	the Tron		
12.	Drummond Street		
13.	Edinburgh		
14.	travelling		
15.	a little deaf		
16.	San Francisco		
17.	Infirmary Street		
18.	not at all		
19.	Drummond Street		
20.	catch twenty-two		
21.	the lantern		
22.	Causewayside		
23.	the lantern		
24.	Chambers Street		
25.	the Tron		

APPENDIX B

You will be played 25 excerpts of recorded conversations. There are usually two speakers, but in a few cases there are three. On the attached pages the text of each excerpt has been typed out. The first person who speaks is Speaker 1, the second who speaks is Speaker 2, and when there is a third speaker he/she is Speaker 3. You will notice that in each excerpt there is one word or a few words which are underlined. You will be asked to decide, after you have listened to the excerpt *whether the underlined part is a question or not*.

Let's take an example. Listen to this excerpt from a conversation between two people:

1 so it depended on whether you passed your exams what school
   you went to
2   oh it did
1   how many years did you go
2 really aye   <u>to school</u>
1 to school after that then
2   oh I left when
1   uh huh
2 I was oh fourteen

The phrase to school (said by the second speaker) is underlined. You have to decide whether this phrase is a question or not. You will be given a sheet with 25 pairs of boxes labelled 'Question' and 'Not-Question'. After listening to each excerpt decide whether the underlined word or words is a question or not and put a tick in the appropriate box with the corresponding number.

Each excerpt will be played to you three successive times. A few seconds before each playing you will hear a warning bleep.

Any questions?

1. 1 where did you go to school
    2   <u>Gillespie's</u>
2. 1 he stays in Dumfries now
    2   oh that's where I come from

    1   oh he's eh married to someone from Dumfries in fact Burwell
    2   no
    1   Jill Burwell no
    2   well I'm from Lockerbie actually
3. 1   have you any brothers or sisters
    2   two younger sisters
4. 1   is that what told you what it was
    2   pardon
    1   is that what gave you the clue
    2   yeah uh-uh
    1   yeah actually it says it's Browns Square
    2   off Chambers Street
    1   yeah do you know where Browns Square is
    2
5. 1   that's is that Georgian architecture
    2   I've no idea
    1   this wee   triangular type thing
    2   I'll ask my father
    3   Old College is Victorian
    1   Victorian that's ah-ha
    2   is it
    3
6. 1   and where were you born
    2   Edinburgh
    1   ah have you lived in Edinburgh all your life
    2
7. 1   I was free till the following Monday then I worked Monday and
    2
    1   Tuesday then I was free till the following Monday again
    2
    1   so it was quite a good break for us
    2   mm
    1   more than usual
    2   especially after working about three shifts a day.
8. 1   any other fascinating drinks that you tried
    2   Mai Tai
    1   yeah
    2   that's another one that's a big fruit cocktail
9. 1   I wonder if you recognise where it is   do you recognise
    2
    1   the lantern   being (points)

```
      2            the lantern          oh that's St Giles
10.   1   where were your parents born
      2                              Haddington East Lothian
                                     both of them
11.   1   is that the Art Gallery at the bottom there
      2                                    mm don't think so
                                           the Tron
      1   the Tron so that's St Giles up there  that's coming down the
          way
      2
12.   1   have you any idea which direction you are looking from
      2
      1   if I say that is St Giles
      2                      Infirmary Street
      1   ehm now where          um hm
      2                    Drummond Street
13.   1   where are you actually getting your examples from all over
      2
      1   Scotland like Caithness Edinburgh where else
      2                                        well  well we're
                                               starting
      1
      2   just in South Edinburgh you see because it's readily available
14.   1   and have you lived in Edinburgh all your life
      2                                        yes
      1   have you moved around at all
      2                          travelling
      1   well from place to place within Edinburgh
      2                                        no no stayed in
      1
      2   Morningside all my life
15.   1   the notion of being a little deaf isn't one that um
      2                                (laugh)     no what would
                                                   you say
      1   a bit deaf       a little deaf     a wee bit deaf
      2         a bit deaf        a wee bit deaf
      1     or pretty deaf      or slightly deaf
      2   ah ha                        oh well
16.   1   were you on your holiday
      2                          yes last summer
      1   where San Francisco
```

2   eh Los Angeles

17. 1 have you any idea which direction you are looking from

      2

      1 if I say that is St Giles   ehm now where

      2   <u>Infirmary Street</u>

      1   uh hum

      2 Drummond Street

18. 1 do you recognise this building   <u>not at all</u> Drummond Street

      2   nope

      1

      2 nope I've got a hell of a memory for streets and I don't recognise

      1 well this   I'll give you a clue this is part of the Old College

      2

19. 1 do you recognise this building   not at all <u>Drummond Street</u>

      2   nope

      1

      2 nope I've got a hell of a memory for streets and I don't recognise

      1 well this   I'll give you a clue this is part of the Old Collge

      2

20. 1 if I don't get the degree I'm unlikely to get a grant um if I get

      2

      1 the degree might not get the grant eh <u>catch twenty-two</u> that's well I

      2

      1 haven't really found out there's one guy who's doing . . .

21. 1 could you have a look at the lower photograph

      2   huh huh

      1 and tell me if you know where it is or where you think it can be

      2

      1 do you recognise the lantern   yep this here (points)

      2   <u>the lantern</u>

      1   yes that's right so it's old Edinburgh

      2 oh yeah St Giles Cathedral

22. 1 right along Melville Drive to the traffic lights turn left

      2

      1 there at eh what on earth's it called <u>Causewayside</u>

      2

      1   Hopepark is it

2 Hopepark Terrace

23. 1 and you should recognise the lantern

2   that's St Giles <u>the lantern</u>

1 yeah this shape of things on the top of St Giles <u>is called</u>

2

1 a lantern

2   ah yeah yeah

24. 1 well it says actually it's Brown Square

2   <u>Chambers Street</u> Brown

1

2 Square Chambers Street really

25. 1 is that the Art Gallery at the bottom there

2   mm don't think so

                                       <u>the Tron</u>

1 the Tron so that's St Giles up there that's <u>coming down the way</u>

2

BIBLIOGRAPHY

Abercrombie, D. 'Syllable Quantity and Enclitics in English' in
    D. Abercrombie, D.B. Fry, P.A.D. McCarthy, N.C. Scott,
    J.L.M. Trim (eds.), *In Honour of Daniel Jones* (Longman, 1964)
——, 'A Phonetician's View of Verse Structure', *Linguistics*, 6 (1964)
Armstrong, L.E. and Ward, I.C. *A Handbook of English Intonation*
    (Cambridge University Press, 1929)
Bolinger, D.L. 'Intonation and Grammar', *Language Learning*, 8 (1958),
    pp. 31-7
——, 'Contrastive Accent and Contrastive Stress', *Language*, 37
    (1961), pp. 83-96
——, 'Contrastive Accent and Contrastive Stress' in I. Abe and
    T. Kanekiyo (eds.), *Forms of English: Accent, Morpheme, Order*,
    (Cambridge, Mass., 1965)
Brazil, D. *An Investigation of Discourse Intonation*, SSRC Project
    HR3316/1, Final Report (1978)
Brown, G. *Listening to Spoken English* (Longman, 1977)
——, 'Understanding Spoken Language', *TESOL Quarterly*, vol. 12,
    no. 3 (1978), pp. 271-83
Brown, P. and Levinson, S. 'Universals in Language Usage: Politeness
    Phenomena' in E.N. Goody (ed.), *Questions and Politeness*
    (Cambridge University Press, 1978)
Burgess, O.N. 'Intonation Patterns in Australian English', *Language and
    Speech*, 16 (1973), pp. 314-26
Chafe, W.L. *Meaning and the Structure of Language* (Chicago
    University Press, 1970)
——, 'Discourse Structure and Human Knowledge' in J.B. Carroll and
    R.O. Freedle (eds.), *Language Comprehension and the Acquisition
    of Knowledge* (John Wiley, 1972)
——, 'Language and Consciousness', *Language*, 50 (1974), pp. 111-33
——, 'Givenness, Contrastiveness, Definiteness, Subjects, Topics and
    Points of View' in C.N. Li (ed.), *Subject and Topic* (Academic Press,
    1976)
Chomsky, N. and Halle, M. *The Sound Pattern of English* (Harper and
    Row, 1968)

Clark, H.H. and Clark, E.V. *Psychology and Language* (Harcourt, Brace, Jovanovich, Inc., 1977)

Coleman, H.O. 'Intonation and Emphasis', *Miscellanea Phonetica*, I (1914), pp. 6-26

Crystal, D. *Prosodic Systems and Intonation in English* (Cambridge University Press, 1969)

———, *The English Tone of Voice* (Arnold, 1975)

Currie, K.L. 'Recent Investigations in Intonation', *Work in Progress*, 11 (Department of Linguistics, University of Edinburgh, 1978)

———, 'Contour Systems in One Variety of Scottish English', *Language and Speech* (1979)

———, 'An Initial Search for Tonics', *Language and Speech* (forthcoming)

———, 'Further Experiments in the "Search for Tonics"', *Work in Progress*, 12 (Department of Linguistics, University of Edinburgh, forthcoming)

Currie, K.L. and Kenworthy, J. 'The Difficulties of Intonation Analysis', *Work in Progress*, 10 (Department of Linguistics, University of Edinburgh, 1977)

Dahl, O. 'What is New Information?' in N.I. Entvist and V. Kohonen (eds.), *Reports on Text Linguistics: Approaches to Word Order* (Text Linguistic Research Group, Abo Akademi, 1976)

Daneš, F. 'Sentence Intonation from a Functional Point of View', *Word*, 16 (1960), pp. 34-54

Denes, P. and Milton-Williams, J. 'Further Studies in Intonation', *Language and Speech*, 5 (1962), pp. 1-14

Fries, C.C. 'On the Intonation of "Yes-No" Questions in English' in D. Abercrombie, D.B. Fry, P.A.D. McCarthy, N.C. Scott, and J.L.M. Trim (eds.), *In Honour of Daniel Jones* (Longman, 1964)

Fry, D.B. 'Experiments in the Perception of Stress', *Language and Speech* 1 (1958), pp. 126-52

Garfinkel, H. *Studies in Ethnomethodology* (Prentice-Hall, New Jersey, 1967)

Garnica, O.K. 'Some Prosodic and Paralinguistic Features of Speech to Young Children' in C.E. Snow and C.A. Ferguson (eds.), *Talking to Children* (Cambridge University Press, 1977)

Gimson, A.C. *An Introduction to the Pronunciation of English* (Arnold, 1959)

Goldmann-Eisler, F. 'The Predictability of Words in Context and the Length of Pauses in Speech', *Language and Speech*, 1 (1958), pp. 226-31

Goody, E.N. (ed.), *Questions and Politeness* (Cambridge University Press, 1978)

——, 'Towards a Theory of Questions' in E.N. Goody (ed.), *Questions and Politeness* (Cambridge University Press, 1978)

Grice, H.P. 'Logic and Conversation' in P. Cole and J. Morgan (eds.), *Syntax and Semantics 3: Speech Acts* (Academic Press, 1975)

Grimes, J.E. *The Thread of Discourse* (Mouton, 1975)

Gunter, R. 'Intonation and Relevance' in D.L. Bolinger (ed.), *Intonation* (Penguin, Harmondsworth, 1972)

Hadding-Koch, K. and Studdert-Kennedy, M. 'An Experimental Study of Some Intonation Contours', *Phonetica*, II (1964), pp. 175-84

——, 'Intonation Contours Evaluated by American and Swedish Test Subjects', *Proceedings of Phonetic Sciences*, V (1965), pp. 326-31

Halliday, M.A.K. 'Phonological (Prosodic) Analysis of the New Chinese Syllable (Modern Pekingese)' in F.R. Palmer (ed.), *Prosodic Analysis* (Oxford University Press, 1970)

——, 'The Tones of English', *Archivum Linguisticum*, XV (1963), pp. 1-28

——, 'Notes on Transitivity and Theme in English', *Journal of Linguistics*, 3 (1967), pp. 177-274

——, *Intonation and Grammar in British English* (Mouton, 1968)

——, *A Course in Spoken English: Intonation* (Oxford University Press, 1970)

t'Hart, J. and Cohen, A. 'Intonation by Rule: A Perceptual Quest', *Journal of Phonetics*, 1 (1973), pp. 309-27

Hudson, R.A. 'The Meaning of Questions', *Language*, 51, no. 1 (1975), pp. 1-31

Hultzen, L.S. 'Information Points in Intonation', *Phonetica*, IV (1959), pp. 107-20

Hymes, D. *Foundations in Sociolinguistics* (University of Pennsylvania Press, 1974)

Jackendoff, R.S. *Semantic Interpretation in Generative Grammar* (Massachusetts Institute of Technology Press, 1972)

Jones, D. *The Pronunciation of English* (Cambridge University Press, 1956)

——, *An Outline of English Phonetics* (Heffer, 1962)

Keenan, E.O. and Schieffelin, B.B. 'Topic as a Discourse Notion: A Study of Topic in the Conversations of Children and Adults' in C.N. Li (ed.), *Subject and Topic* (Academic Press, 1976)

Kenworthy, J. 'The Intonation of Questions in One Variety of Scottish English', *Work in Progress*, 10 (Department of Linguistics, University of Edinburgh, 1977)

——, 'The Intonation of Questions in One Variety of Scottish English', *Lingua*, 44 (1978), pp. 267-82

Kingdon, R. *The Groundwork of English Intonation* (Longman, 1958)

Ladefoged, P. *A Course in Phonetics* (Harcourt, Brace, Jovanovich, Inc., 1975)

Laver, J.D.M. 'Voice Quality and Indexical Information', *British Journal of Disorders of Communication*, 3, no. 1 (1968), pp. 43-55

Lehiste, I. *Suprasegmentals* (Cambridge, Mass., 1970)

Li, C.N. (ed.), *Subject and Topic* (Academic Press, 1976)

Lieberman, P. 'On the Acoustic Basis of the Perception of Intonation by Linguists', *Word*, 21 (1965), pp. 40-54

——, *Intonation, Perception and Language* (Massachusetts Institute of Technology Press, 1967)

Lyons, J. *Introduction to Theoretical Linguistics* (Cambridge University Press, 1968)

——, *Semantics*, vol. 1 (Cambridge University Press, 1977)

Morton, J. and Jassem, W. 'Acoustic Correlates of Stress', *Language and Speech*, 8 (1965), pp. 159-81

O'Connor, J.D. and Arnold, G.F. *Intonation of Colloquial English* (Longman, 1959)

Ohala, J.J. 'The Production of Tone', *Report of the Phonology Laboratory*, no. 2 (University of California, Berkeley, 1978), pp. 63-116

Palmer, H.E. *English Intonation* (Heffer, 1922)

Peterson, G.E. and Lehiste, I. 'Duration of Syllable Nuclei in English', *Journal of the Acoustical Society of America*, 32 (1960), pp. 693-703

Pike, K.L. *The Intonation of American English* (University of Michigan Press, 1945)

Quirk, R., Greenbaum, S., Leech, G. and Svartvik, J. *A Grammar of Contemporary English* (Longman, 1972)

Schmerling, S.F. 'A Re-examination of "Normal Stress" ', *Language*, 50 (1974), pp. 66-73

Searle, J.R. *Speech Acts* (Cambridge University Press, 1969)

Stevens, S.S. and Volkman, J. 'The Relation of Pitch to Frequency: A Revised Scale', *The American Journal of Psychology*, vol. 53, no. 3 (1940), pp. 329-53

Stevens, S.S., Volkman, J. and Newman, E.B. 'A Scale for the Measurement of the Psychological Magnitude of Pitch', *Journal of the Acoustical Society of America*, 8 (1937), pp. 185-90

Sweet, H. *A Primer of Phonetics* (Clarendon Press, 1906)

Trager, G.L. and Smith, H.L. Jr *An Outline of English Structure*, Studies in Linguistics, Occasional Papers 3 (Battenburg Press, 1951)

Trubetzkoy, N.S. *Principles of Phonology*, translated by C.A.M. Baltaxe (University of California Press, 1969)

Uldall, E. 'Dimensions of Meaning in Intonation' in D. Abercrombie, D.B. Fry, P.A.D. McCarthy, N.C. Scott, J.L.M. Trim (eds.), *In Honour of Daniel Jones* (Longman, 1964)

Van Dijk, T.A. *Text and Context* (Longman, 1977)

Welmers, W.E. 'Tonemics, Morphotonemics and Tonal Morphemes', *General Linguistics*, 4 (1959), pp. 1-9

Yule, G. 'Intonation and Ambiguity', *The Intonation of Scottish English* (SSRC Report HR3601, 1979) (forthcoming)

AUTHOR INDEX

SUBJECT INDEX